After retiring in 1991 as a United Methodist pastor, Stanley C. Brown continued his avocation of research and writing regional history. For thirty years his family had a summer home on the upper East Verde River, which stimulated his fascination with the prehistoric and historic stories of the Rim Country. In 1993 he and his wife Ruth made their permanent home in Payson, and for twelve years he was appointed by the Town of Payson as its official historian. He served a number of years on the board of directors for the Northern Gila County Historical Society, including a time as its president, and developed the first historical archive for the Rim Country Museum. He has written weekly and bi-weekly columns for the *Payson Roundup* and has had numerous papers published in the *Journal of Arizona History*. His books and a historical novel are available at the museum. In 2004 the Browns moved to Arizona's first territorial capital, Prescott, where Stan continues his research and writing.

A FRONTIER TEACHER IN TONTO BASIN

The 1880 Diary of Angeline Mitchell

Edited by Stanley C. Brown

Copyright 2014 by Stanley C. Brown
Published 2014 by Rim Country Press
2nd printing 2016
Northern Gila County Historical Society, Inc.
P.O. Box 2432, Payson, AZ 85547
Tel: 928-474-3483
www.rimcountrymuseums.com

TABLE OF CONTENTS

INTRODUCTION 1

1. The Most Barbaric Country — 12
2. Wild Ride to Rye Creek — 16
3. Arrival in Tonto Basin — 21
4. Introduction to Pioneer Life — 26
5. The Move to Lower Tonto — 31
6. School Begins on the Lower Tonto — 36
7. A Mountain Lion Tries to Get In — 41
8. Life Settles in to Routine — 46
9. Attack by Apache Warriors — 50
10. Escape From the Apache — 55
11. Cowboys Confront the Apaches — 69
12. Skunks and Cattle Stampedes — 75
13. A Typical Weekend in Tonto Basin — 80
14. An Invasion of Harer Family Members — 85
15. How to Build a Pole House — 91
16. A Gila Monster Comes to School — 97
17. A Hike Almost Ends in Disaster — 103
18. Early Visitors to Tonto Cliff Dwellings — 108
19. Preparations to Leave Tonto — 117
20. A Visit with Captain and Mrs. Chaffee — 122
21. A Race to Get Home for Christmas — 129
22. A Frightful Final Ride — 135
23. Epilogue, The Wedding — 140

Photographic Credits — 147
Index — 148
Map

A FRONTIER TEACHER IN TONTO BASIN
The 1880 Diary of Angeline Mitchell
edited by Stanley C. Brown

INTRODUCTION

A young, educated woman, Angie Mitchell arrived in Prescott, Arizona Territory with her parents and brother in November 1875. Her diary, in her neat longhand, is in the library archives of the Sharlot Hall Museum in Prescott, Arizona. The first of her diary excerpts is dated December 22, 1876. She wrote on a dated scrap of paper: "The Christmas Tree on the plaza was cut down on the night of Dec 22 by some unknown person."

A squib in the *Weekly Miner* dated that same day gives us something of the flavor of this frontier town. It further described the anger of the community over this incident, "A DISGUSTED COMMUNITY – More than two-thirds of the citizens of Prescott are mad, sad and disgusted over the action of the town council in cutting down several noble pines that ornamented the southeast corner of the plaza. Going downtown this afternoon our attention was directed to several prostrate monarchs of the forest which had just been cut down. We felt sad since we had known them since 1874. We recollected how John Tatman and several other brave pioneers – some of whom are now in their graves – had reclined beneath the branches of those great trees; how our people had prided themselves upon the natural shade and beauty they used to shed upon the town; how strangers visiting the Village, a name to which Prescott is justly entitled, used to admire those departed plaza ornaments, and our feeling of sadness gave way to one of disgust for the act of vandalism. The pathetic appeal, `Woodman spare that tree' must have been entirely forgotten by those who ordered the commitment of the act, which has caused so much regret in our community. Yesterday almost everybody was, at heart, in favor of keeping up the town government; today the feeling is quite different; but we hope they will overlook this one bad act and not permit it to have any influence over them when they come to vote on the question of incorporation or dis-incorporation."

Angie's diary proper begins soon after this on January 1, 1877. However, to set the scene we first look briefly at 19th century life in Prescott. An eyewitness picture of Prescott in 1877 is furnished by Hiram C. Hodge in his 1877 book, *Arizona As It Is: The Coming Country*," page 147f. He lists the population of Yavapai County at 13,738, one-half the population of the entire Territory. "Prescott, the county town, by an act of the Territorial Legislature, January 1877, once more made the capital of the Territory, is as beautiful a mountain town as can be found on the Pacific slope. It has a population of 3,800, consisting almost wholly of white people of the better class. It is surrounded by mountains on all sides, which are covered with forests of pine and other timber. The town is well laid out on the eastern side of Granite Creek, one of the tributaries of the Verde River."

"An addition has been laid out by Judge Fleury, on the western side of Granite Creek, which adds much to the beauty and growth of the town. The Judge is an old and respected resident, and came to the Territory in 1863 with Governor Goodwin and suite, and took part in the organization of the Territory, and has been identified with Arizona and its interests, and especially with Yavapai County ever since. A beautiful plaza adds much to the beauty of the town, being in its center, and surrounded on all sides with fine business blocks, residences etc."

"There are fourteen mercantile houses in town, three jewelers, three meat markets, four livery stables, three breweries, eight carpenter shops, eight blacksmith shops, seven wagon shops, five hotels and restaurants, five boot and shoe stores, fourteen saloons, two tin shops, two barbers, seven attorneys, four physicians, one drug store, four milliners, one dentist, one harness shop, one photographic gallery, three assay offices, one extensive sash, door and blind factory, one church edifice, Methodist… There is also a comfortable county court-house and jail, and good county offices, and an excellent new brick schoolhouse, erected at a cost of $12,000, and capable of accommodating three hundred pupils, with Professor Sherman, Principal, and a good corps of assistants… This past year Prescott reported over $500,000 of gold and silver bullion, 350,000 pounds of wool, and a large amount of lumber and other products…"

Life there did not lack entertainment; dances, or "balls," were common. The local newspaper announces one such event in the spring of 1876, while Angie was still at home with her parents.

May 12, 1876, *Prescott Weekly Miner* – "Remember Professor Fischer's Grand Concert and Ball to-night, at Campbell & Mee's Hall. The ball will be given immediately after the concert closes. One dollar buys a ticket to the concert, and those who desire to attend the ball, will present their invitation cards and be charged a dollar extra for that privilege. Children under ten-years of age can attend the concert for half price. "

On the following day the paper mentions Angie Mitchell among others as attending the "Concert and Ball."

May 13, 1876, *Weekly Miner*,: "Professor Fischer's Concert: The concert and ball given by Professor Fischer on Saturday night last, gave entire satisfaction to the large audience that crowded Campbell and Mee's Hall. Want of space prevents us from noticing, as we should, Miss Williams, Mrs. Raible, Miss Mitchell, and Messrs Pattibone, Kelley and DeJarnae, who each contributed so materially to the pleasure of the occasion."

Regarding entertainment in Prescott, Angie makes extensive references to visitation in homes, attendance at plays and musicals, and attending church to hear specific preachers. The evaluations of sermons rendered in the diary suggest that going to church was among the forms of entertainment. There were two Methodist congregations in Prescott at this time, Methodist Episcopal Church on Marina Street, meeting in the first Protestant church building erected in Arizona Territory, and the Methodist Episcopal Church, South, meeting in a new building erected in December 1876 west of Granite Creek. This was near the Mitchell home, and Angie became a member of this church. She played the organ for services.

A Methodist revival in the community, reported in the *Miner, March 3, 1876*, indicated the attraction of such events, "Revs. Groves and Hedgpeth have successfully conducted a mission here for a term of 14 days, and succeeded in awakening a greater interest in religious matters than was ever before known in Yavapai County. The last Sunday night was crowned with greater success than had attended their efforts before, and it was thought they might easily have kept up the interest a week longer. The house was so crowded on Sunday night that many had to go away for want of standing room, and eight persons joined the church, making sixteen in all during the continuance of the meetings. These were mostly strangers to us but from their appearances we judge them to be earnest Christians and good citizens. By reference to our subscription lists, where majority of permanent residents of the County have their names enrolled, we fail to discover any of theirs, therefore we conclude they must be strangers."

The following month, April 1876, a Presbyterian congregation was organized and met in the Methodist church. In August Rev. J. A. Merrill arrived to be the pastor to the Presbyterian members. His name appears regularly in Angie's diary over the next few years, indicating her appreciation of his ministry.

Angie's first teaching assignment awaited her certification by the Yavapai County school examiners and is dated October 2, 1876. With this hurdle cleared, she was hired by the Walnut Grove School, a mining and ranching community over the Bradshaw Mountains southwest of Prescott. The following announcement appeared in the paper.

Oct 16, 1876, *Weekly Miner*, "Letter from Walnut Grove, Cottonwood Camp: The public school of this district is now open and is well attended. Miss Mitchell, formerly of Prescott, is the teacher. From what I hear of the lady, the trustees are to be congratulated in having secured the services of one so thoroughly competent. It is the intention in a short time to erect a more commodious and comfortable building than one now in use."

A word is in order about Angie Mitchell's family, whose arrival was prompted by a job opportunity offered to her father. The sale of land to early settlers by the town of Prescott, Arizona Territory, was illegal because the undesignated town site was still under the jurisdiction of the federal government. After the United States Congress set the town apart from federal lands a territorial judge took possession of the town site and a new survey was required. Daniel F. Mitchell of Kansas, a civil engineer and surveyor by trade, answered the call for surveyors and teachers and brought his family to Prescott. He earned their way by joining with a group called The Arizona Mining Association as the company engineer. Anson W. Callen organized the group and the families of company members traveled together.

Daniel F. Mitchell was born in Bridgewater, Massachusetts, February 7, 1807 and he followed his early interests to become a civil engineer and surveyor. After his first wife died he married Angeline Brigham and she became stepmother for his two sons, William D. and Daniel Francis Mitchell. Angeline gave birth to a daughter on October 5, 1854. They named her after her mother, Angeline Brigham Mitchell, and called her "Angie." Mrs. Mitchell was the principle schoolteacher at Brattleboro Vermont Academy until Daniel moved the family to Ogden, Kansas in 1857. In 1858 Daniel served as surveyor for the town site of Junction City, Kansas. The family followed him there in 1861 after the U. S. Land Office employed him as an engineer and an attorney. Mrs. Mitchell taught school in a log cabin and was becoming a well known writer. Her articles would appear in Harpers Young Folks, Mothers Journal, Youth Companion, and Home Journal.

Angie followed her mother's example as a writer and a brilliant student. After being educated in the public schools at age 15 she attended Kansas State Agricultural College at Manhattan from September 1869 to March 1872. She then attended the University of

Kansas at Lawrence until June 1873 and obtained a teaching certificate. Angie taught school in various Kansas communities until June of 1875 when she joined her family in the move to Arizona and arrived here in November 1875.

Angie's brother, Daniel F. Mitchell, became a prominent photographer in Prescott. The other Mitchell son, William, had studied to be an engineer like his father, but the Civil War intervened and he served both in the Kansas Volunteers and the U. S. Cavalry. William was killed in battle in North Carolina March 10, 1865, and Mitchell County, Kansas was named in his memory.

After coming to Arizona, Mrs. Mitchell served on the Territorial Board of Examiners for Teachers. She died July 21, 1907 in the home of her daughter and son-in-law near Phoenix, where she had been living. The death of Angie's father in July 1877 is recorded in her diary.

By the time of the move to Arizona, Angie was 21 and in October 1876 she obtained a certificate to teach in Yavapai County. For the next three years she taught three and four month terms in the schools of Walnut Grove, Tiger Mine, Chino Valley and Miller Valley. These were rural and mountain settings surrounding her family's home in Prescott. The diary she kept during these years reveals her gift as a keen observer and proficient writer.

Her life in the Territorial Capital of Prescott was quite sophisticated, hobnobbing with political and community leaders, sermon tasting in Prescott's first churches, attending plays and concerts, dancing and spending countless evenings visiting with her peers. In the autumn of 1880 she took the teaching position in Tonto Basin. There she was thrust into a most primitive frontier style of life and encountered cattle stampedes, skunk attacks, Gila monsters, crude strangers, and raiding Apaches. Her descriptions of life in this isolated area of the Territory are perhaps the best example we can find of settlement at that time. Her vivid descriptions of customs, family inter-relationships, transportation, building pole houses, the interior of these crude homes, and the architecture of prehistoric cliff dwellings give unique insight into frontier life.

Angie's writings are contained in a collection of Mitchell/Brown papers in the archives of the Sharlot Hall Museum, in Prescott, Arizona. Among these papers, and not included in this book, is an extensive listing of the clothing and personal possessions she had throughout her college years and a description of classes, professors, dormitory rooms and courses of study. Angie was intensely curious about the many prehistoric ruins found throughout Yavapai County and did not hesitate to collect artifacts from these sites, listing them and their locations. This was prior to federal regulations about such things. She gave most of her acquisitions to museums and friends.

We found no diary for 1875 or 1876 and very few entries for 1877. However, written notes from 1877 to the first half of 1879 appear on miscellaneous pages and are preserved in the collection, anonymously cut and pasted on larger sheets as in a scrapbook. We have assembled all of these in chronological order. While this book relates only to her Tonto Basin sojourn we have edited the entire diary elsewhere. Her diaries from 1879 to 1880 appear in bound journals and are quite consistent. Of interest is a parallel diary by her close friend Josie Stephens, also found in the Sharlot Hall Museum archive. When Angie's diary skips days during the period from March 1879 to September 1880 we have included entries from Josie's diary. Josie seems to have been influenced by her friend to keep a diary and when Angie prepares to move to Tonto Basin Josie's diary stops.

  The format of the diary proper includes footnotes to clarify terms she has used that may be obscure to the reader. The day of the week for each entry is included where she has written it, but for most entries she did not write the day of the week. In those cases we have included the correct day in brackets. Some of her misspelling has been left as she wrote it (such as "staid" for "stayed"), and gross errors are usually noted with "sic." Her sentences are often endless, connected by a series of conjunctions, and for clarity we have occasionally inserted a period. Her punctuation includes a "dash" for a "period," or a lack of capital letters and she often splits her infinitives. With only occasional adjustments, we have left her sentence structure as she wrote it. When the local newspaper, *The Miner*, had an article relating to an event in the diary we have inserted it with her entry. Nearly all of these, however, are to be found in the longer editing.

Women in frontier America have intrigued historians and readers for their bravery as well as for the balance their femininity brought to the expanding west. Angie Mitchell fits nobly into this genre. Her beautiful handwriting and fluid descriptive style made this enterprise a distinct pleasure. For our purposes, her diary begins in the summer of 1880.

Chapter 1
The Most Barbaric Country

It had been raining "awfully" the morning of Tuesday September 14, 1880. Because of the weather Angie Mitchell and her fiancé, George Brown, didn't leave Prescott until nearly two o'clock that afternoon. The two, along with Angie's mother, Angeline Brigham Mitchell, were heading east over the Mogollon Rim to the Tonto Basin where she was under contract to become that area's first teacher.

Her application for the job was made to spite her boyfriend. On September 5th, nine days before their departure from Prescott, she wrote in her diary, "George went downtown about 10 and found out from Dan O'Leary and St. James concerning the Tonto Road, then came back at 12 and said things about my craziness in wanting to go to such an out of the way place. I merely reminded him that I promised him I'd go to the most barbaric country I could if he ran for anything on the ticket. He promised not to and I abandoned my intention of going to St. Johns, Apache County; that he broke his share of the agreement and I thought Tonto would answer my purpose nearly as well as St. Johns. "

George Brown was elected to the 11th Territorial Legislature.

Angie continues, "I hoped he'd be willing to take me (to Tonto), but if he wasn't I'd go to Phoenix by stage and get some way to going to Tonto Basin from there. He looked disgusted, but the whole thing is a little amusing. We both laughed, and he said he'd assuredly take me if I was going anyhow."

The previous month she wrote, "August 31, Tuesday. Applied to W. A. Hancock for Tonto School."

The mail service was very good with stage coaches running regularly between Prescott and the Phoenix-Mesa communities. It was the following Saturday Angie had her answer from the superintendent of schools for Maricopa County.

"September 4, Saturday. Letter from Hancock. He says I can have the school. Applied to Sherman for Territorial Certificate..." [1] She would soon have occasion to encounter Superintendent Hancock in another context. He first appeared in Territorial history as a 2nd lieutenant commanding an army detachment in 1865 that was raiding Apache camps in the Tonto Basin. While searching an abandoned camp in the foothills of the Sierra Ancha he discovered a one-hundred-dollar legal tender note in the ruins of a collapsed Apache *wickiup*. This gave rise to naming the site Greenback Valley. After leaving the army Hancock went on in various roles; superintendent of the farm at Camp McDowell, Justice of the Peace in Phoenix, a trader at Camp Reno. His lasting marks were made as a civil engineer in the Salt River Valley, building the first house and store in Phoenix, being appointed the first sheriff of Maricopa County in 1871, and then serving as postmaster for Phoenix. He also served as a district attorney, coroner, probate judge, and the county's first superintendent of schools. During his career in Phoenix he became good friends with the David Harer family which was looking for a place to homestead. Hancock pointed them to Greenback Valley on the stream of the same name that was a tributary of Tonto Creek. That is where the Harers settled and as their family grew, along with those of other settlers, David Harer built the first school in the Basin along Tonto Creek and hired a teacher – Angie Mitchell. Hancock would meet her on a visit to his friends the Harers.

Angie, having been hired and receiving her credentials, put in a frantic ten days getting ready for her adventure. "September 6, Monday. Washed my duds, then sorted trunk and boxes for Tonto. Can only take a little trunk and it is hard to decide what I can do without. Mother will go with us and she is merely resigned not jubilant. Really, one would think I was going to the Feegee (sic) Isles."

Her mother and friends were "resigned" only after they had done all they could to persuade her to stay home, suggesting she start a "select school" with paying pupils. At first she agreed to try. "I got 12 without any trouble and was actually scared lest I'd get 3 more. Time favored me and I couldn't get any more positively promised, though I honestly did my best, and so that settled it."

The Prescott *Weekly Miner*, September 14, 1880, published the following about one of their favorite local ladies. "Miss Angie Mitchell has gone to teach the school in Tonto Basin. The people of that new and thriving community could not have made a better selection. Miss Mitchell is an experienced and accomplished teacher, and we congratulate the Trustees of Tonto District on their good judgment as well as good fortune in securing her services."

"September 14, Tuesday. I intended to start early but it rained awfully, and we did not get off till nearly 2. George has Andy M(iles)'s durable spring wagon and his own team Mug and Charlie. Ma, George and I got to Hance's at 9." Angie Mitchell could not know that she was setting out on the most harrowing journey of her life.

NOTES:

[1] Moses H. Sherman was the principal of the Arizona Territory's first graded school, the Prescott Free Academy, which opened in 1876. In 1879 Sherman was appointed Territorial School Superintendent by Governor Fremont. Since Maricopa County was beyond Angie's Yavapai County teaching credentials she needed a Territorial Certificate.

Chapter 2
Wild Ride to Rye Creek

The young teacher, Angie Mitchell, was on her way from the comforts of the Territorial Capital in Prescott to the unknown settlement of Tonto Basin. She was accompanied by her mother and her fiancé, George Brown, who drove an overloaded spring wagon. The first leg of their trip found them spending the night at the ranch of George and Parthena Hance in Camp Verde. He had been one of the earliest settlers in the Verde Valley and was the local Justice of the Peace. Like so many frontier families they provided an overnight stop where travelers could be refreshed - an early day "Bed and Breakfast."

The next day they followed the Crook Military Road east from Camp Verde and it was extremely steep. That night they camped on top of Government Hill about half way to the top of the Mogollon Rim and near the 13-mile marker on the Crook Trail that can be visited today just off highway 260.

Angie writes, "September 16, Thursday, Rained all night but our camp was high and dry among the cedars and our impoverished tent kept us dry and comfortable (Ma and I) while George fared equally well in the wagon. Got up early and found the sun shining over the mountains. Ate a hearty breakfast and started on. Went to Mud Tanks about 4 miles over a fearful road. [1] There George fed and watered the horses and we started again. Only went about a mile when a big black cloud came overhead and promised to hail us out of existence. In a jiffy George unhitched the train and in two jiffies fixed a shelter under the wagon for us. The storm passed by us and we only got a very little of it, and were thankful. Then we went to Government Wells and camped for the night."

Government Wells is a name commonly used on trails in America and it is difficult to identify exactly where they were, but it was a restless night. "September 17, Friday, Ma sick with cramp colic part of the night. (She was) all right today. Also had bad pain in her lungs so I did her up in mustard, rubbed her in liniment and dosed her with hot whiskey and she got better…" Angie was well prepared with various treatments for sickness as one had to be in the wilderness.

At the top of The Rim they left the Crook Trail and went south over the Rim to the village of Strawberry. That required a drop of at least one thousand feet and was on the trail over Nash Point. It was named for the homesteader at its base; in the 1870s settlers coming from the north sought out the gentlest route they could find. There had been a faint Indian trail which was widened but the wagons had to drag large pine logs behind them as brakes so they did not overrun the horses.

"…Then to Pine Creek and camped at the Mormon's ranch. This man has 2 or else 3 wives and we saw 16 children sitting on some logs. They seemed to be nearly the same age and size, and looked exactly alike – about as wild as quail. There are also an assorted variety of dogs and one of them laying down near the wagon had a tick or something on its back. As it tried to scratch it off it kept up a funny grunting noise that sounded, ma said, exactly as if he was swearing. It was ridiculous. Tonight after the cows were milked the 16 twins and about as many older ones each with a bowl of bread and milk scattered around the yard and ate their suppers. George says he counted them and there were 73, but he exaggerates a trifle, though there really are 22 or 23 of the kids. But I don't suppose they belong to one family."

  The next morning, Saturday September 18, "the Mormon Father directed us, I presume correctly, how to get to Green Valley. But another Mormon, Fuller, arrived during the night and he chipped in and gave other directions and told us to follow his wagon track to East Fork of Verde, and from there it would be a straight, plain road to Green Valley."

  It is helpful for those not familiar with the history of Pine to know that the community is deeply rooted in a Mormon heritage and is inseparable from the family name of Fuller. The patriarch, Elijah Knapp Fuller, sent three of his sons in 1878-79 to settle at the mouth of Pine Creek where it joins the East Verde River. Others joined them but because of danger from Apache attacks all but a few of the Mormon families moved north along Pine Creek to its headwaters under the Rim where they established the community of Pine. It is not possible to identify which of the homesteads in the Pine area became Angie and George's campsite that night.

Their original plan had been to follow the trail to Green Valley (in 1884 Green Valley would become Payson) along the general route taken by today's Highway 87 from Pine. Apparently, after the rancher directed them "correctly" to Green Valley one of the Fullers from the community at the mouth of Pine Creek suggested it was shorter for them to go south along the creek to the East Verde where his ranch was located and then follow a well-used army trail into Green Valley. The Mitchell party assumed that since either way had to cross the East Verde it would be okay to take the suggested shorter route.

They started out in their "well loaded" spring wagon pulled by "two medium sized horses… The track led over a country that was well-nigh impassable for us, and in one place we drove for a long ways along the side of a steep mountain, with no road, only a kind of rut marked for the upper wheel to follow and at an angle that it seemed as if no one could drive. We got out. George took off the halters and some harness straps and pieced them together the best he could. Then tied them around the wagon in some shape and gave me one with the instructions to walk leaning uphill and keep the line taut if I could. But be sure to let go if it started to go over the canyon side, 75 feet or more to the bottom. He held the front one and drove the horses that seemed to sense the danger and did their best. Ma walked a safe distance from us. Twice it almost went and if George had not repacked the wagon putting trunk, bedding, seat etc. all the way on the upper edge and tying them there, the thing would surely have gone."

When they looked over the edge of the canyon they saw "the total wreck of what had been at some time a loaded freight wagon, the bones and hides of four horses, and parts of the harness."

When they finally got that harrowing experience behind them they spent another half hour repacking the wagon and adjusting the harnesses. "We traveled over a horrid road till just after dark we came to what seemed to be the jumping off place of all Creation, but found it to be the mountain overlooking the (East) Verde River."

They went down "like going down the side of a steep roof," dragging a log behind them to act as a brake. "Once down we discovered we were in a bowl-like valley which had only one tiny log house in it. We went there and the woman looked at us in amazement as she asked, `How on earth did you get in here in that rig and where are you going?'"

NOTES:

[1] Mud Tanks was a spring located on the Mogollon Rim at a junction with several other trails. The elevation is 6,250 feet so they still had a thousand foot climb ahead of them.

Chapter 3
Arrival in Tonto Basin

The harrowing ride down Pine Creek had almost cost the Mitchells the loss of their wagon, team and belongings; perhaps even their lives. Mrs. Fuller was startled to see them. Upon telling her their goal was Tonto Basin she informed them they could not possibly get there from here and would have to go back. "That was quite too much for my worn out nerves," wrote Angie in her diary that evening of September 18th. "I said, `Very well, I shall live and die here (rather) than go back over that awful mountainside; I never will', and added that if I only had that contemptible sneak who sent us in here where I could talk to him just ten minutes I should be perfectly happy!"

The astounded ranch wife answered, "Poor child, no wonder you feel so. He is my husband and it's not the first trick he played on people, though I believe it is one of the meanest I've ever known him to do."

To unsettle them even more she informed them that the wreck they saw "at the bottom of the canyon was one of their wagons loaded with their household truck that had gone to the bottom the autumn before when they were moving in and that two of the family jumped for it, barely in time to save themselves, and that 3 horses out of the 6 attached to it were killed, and two more crippled so they had to be shot, and scarcely any baggage could be saved as it all was ground to kindling wood." Angie felt breathless as she wrote this, the anxiety of the previous day returned full force.

Mrs. Fuller apologized that she could not keep them in the house that night but showed them a good place to camp nearby. Then she sent her children out with hot biscuits and milk. The Mitchells put up the tent for Angie. Her mother then arranged their blankets for the night and George slept under the wagon. They sat around their campfire "wondering how upon earth we would ever get over that road again," when the Fuller's oldest boy, about 13, came out with good news. He had come home from bringing in cattle and when his mother told him the plight of their overnight guests he reminded her that there was a road down Wild Rye Creek and he could show it to them. It was a road he had taken with his father when they went to a mill for flour.

The lad came out to the Mitchell camp and reported this good news. They would not have to go into Green Valley after all because Wild Rye Creek would take them to their destination. It flows in a southeasterly direction until it enters Tonto Creek. [1]

"Sunday September 19. Well! Such a night. Thorns and cat claws will never make a downy bed and that is all the sort of grass their fine ranch seems to afford." Angie's mother called the mattresses they put together "Verde feathers" and in their restlessness during the night the women could hear George swearing under the wagon.

The next morning the Fuller boy guided them across the East Verde River and down along the bed of Rye Creek until they came to "a canyon-like place." He assured them they would not get lost because they could not get out of the canyon until they reached "Nelson's place 14 miles away."

The Nelson Price family had settled where the road from Green Valley came over Ox Bow Hill and met the trail to Tonto Basin. The crossroad was simply called Rye. Although the Nelson Prices had moved to Pine in 1878 their ranch still carried the family name. The Mitchells reached there just at sunset and made camp about a half-mile from the ranch house "thankful to be alive." It had been a rough ride.

Angie describes the day's travel. "It was impossible for Ma to stand the jolting she said, and George said he'd walk too for the load was pretty heavy for the teams over such boulders. I offered to walk and let either of them drive, but Ma said, `My gracious, I wouldn't attempt to drive through this inferno for a fortune,' and George said (to me), `You are better in the wagon than I for the lighter the load the better.' I weigh 105 and he about 160 and Ma 164. I drove and may I never again have such a road to drive, though it is far preferable to yesterday's in point of danger."

She reported that for the entire 14 miles one wheel never touched the ground because of the "rocks of all sizes and kinds. Monday, September 20. We had a good night's rest and started early for Blake's."

Angie had been given the name of the family they were to contact in Tonto Basin. Two brothers, Andrew and John Blake (both born in Scotland), had settled on the lower stretch of Rye Creek. John was single and although at this time he had been elected local Justice of the Peace he apparently did not remain long in Tonto Basin.

Andrew Blake had married Narsisses Jane Harer, the daughter of settler David Harer, and this couple would become significant figures in Angie's support group. [2]

Angie continued her entry regarding their last day on the trail to Tonto Basin. "Camped for dinner in a lovely place 10 miles from Nelson's and at sunset reached Judge John Blake's, 8 miles from noon camp. We found the Judge and his brother Andrew and wife Janie very pleasant and kind and expecting me. But school can't begin for a week so I'm to rest up here. This is not a very cheerful place to put it mildly. But the people will do all they can to make us comfortable." [3]

For the next five days Angie remained at the Blake ranch waiting for the school and her "teacherage" to be prepared farther down on Tonto Creek. Her first night at Blake's held some excitement. "September 21. A long hot night. Ma and I slept on a floor in the front room. George as usual under the wagon outside. Some freighters are camped on the other side. About midnight two big bulls got into a fight, and one drove the other straight toward the house, which is adobe and might easily sustain a serious damage if such a wedge was driven against it. The men outside yelled to us inside to `get out and be quick as one would have the other driven there in a minute.' We surely `got.' A sick man was in one of the wagons and he watched the fight, but the bulls just grazed the corner of the house and passed straight towards that wagon, and my! Didn't he get out of there in a hurry! The men belabored the bulls with poles and everything they could get hold of but they paid not the least attention to them. Finally they got out on the mesa still fighting and everyone returned to sleep."

NOTES:

[1] Wild Rye Creek was named by the army in the 1860s because of the wild grasses that grow along its banks.
[2] An undated clipping from *The Tempe News* in the Sharlot Hall Museum obituary collection reported that "a Mrs. Andrew Blake of Tonto Basin has committed suicide by shooting herself."
[3] The Blake ranch was most likely where the more recent Brown Ranch is located above "the Narrows" on Rye Creek before it enters Tonto Creek.

Chapter 4
Introduction to Pioneer Life

The Mitchell family's second day in Tonto Basin was one of leisure. George and "Ma" had planned to begin their return trip to Prescott but after he hitched up the wagon that morning he "concluded to our surprise that he was too tired to go home." It was Wednesday September 22, 1880. Andy Blake suggested that they all go fishing and taking a wagon they "all went up Tonto three or four miles to some pools." Angie actually means they went up Rye Creek, but in that early day many still called Rye Creek a branch of Tonto Creek and the main branch of the Tonto was called "the North Fork."

"While Mrs. Blake and I were sitting pretty near the wall of the canyon in the shade talking and watching the three men on rocks in a pool fishing, mother had climbed up the canyon lower down and gone to gathering flowers."

This description sounds as though they were in "The Narrows," which would mean they had gone downstream instead of up. There is a canyon there where Rye Creek cuts through and since the 1920s it has been bridged by a one-lane steel bridge. It is this location where one of the Apache families had their traditional camp site and where the late Tonto Apache Chief Melton Campbell was born. However, in 1880 the Apaches were all incarcerated on the San Carlos

Reservation and would return to this area about ten years later.

What happened to Angie next was one of those many events in the Tonto Basin she would long remember. Her mother, gathering flowers, "was just above us, some 30 or 40 feet, where the wall is nearly straight and was calling down to us, when her foot struck a rock as big as a hen's egg. It of course fell over the edge. A second passed and a shriek from Mrs. Blake scared all of them. They turned and saw me stretched out as if I was dead. Everybody on the rocks came running to shore, and Ma nearly fell over the cliff in her hurry. They flung water in my face and in a minute I sat up and gasped, `Why did you throw that rock at me?'

"I was sitting with my head bent a little forward looking at a curious rock I had picked up. That small rock Ma dislodged had fallen and struck me a terrible blow, first under the shoulder blade and close to the spine. It had knocked the breath out of me and made me feel faint for a minute. Ma presently arrived to see what ailed me and was astonished to know that she was the innocent cause of all the commotion. After that they all fished but me, and I was too lame to care to. About dusk we went home." That evening Angie and George, along with her mother, Andy and Janie Blake walked "around the place." She commented, "Such magnificent moonlight nights." George and Ma did start their journey home the next day, Thursday September 23rd. They went the way they had originally planned their trip, returning to Green Valley and then following the road to Pine and Strawberry. That evening as Angie made her diary entry she described her pangs of loneliness in unfamiliar surroundings.

"Today for the first time in my life I know what it is to feel utterly cast away and homesick. This is isolation itself here, high frowning hills, a long stretch of dusty road, no fields, no trees except a few near what is a creek part of the year. No shade near the house, no porch around it..."

Then she proceeds to describe the interior of the Blake's primitive home. For the young lady who had known relative luxury all her life, it was all quite shocking. "No furniture in it except a broken cook stove; two shaky tables, a rough board bedstead, 3 or 4 homemade camp stools, an almanac and 3 or 4 papers a month old. A law book and book of forms; ½ dozen plates, 3 saucers, 2 cups and 3 or 4 tin cups, 3 or 4 tin plates; steel knives and forks, a tin cup to hold sugar, a tin cup for salt and lard buckets to cook in. (There is) a gourd dipper, an old tin water pail and ditto milk pail, a nice new style churn; 2 old battered tubs, a broom, and a rough bench; a dozen good milk pans, a piece of tin with holes punched for a skimmer, and a lot of iron and tin spoons assorted sizes all ages, constitute the household goods of this family. I'm not slurring them. I'm simply filled with amazement that people, sensible, nice people can live in such a way! Oh yes, there's a block with 3 nails in it for one candle stick and a bottle for another. The beds are ticks filled with hay; the pillows about the same, hard anyway and there's only one. Heavens! Will my boarding place be a duplicate?"

The next day Angie went exploring on her own and pursued one of her favorite hobbies, exploring prehistoric ruins. As in most of Arizona, Tonto Basin is rife with the artifacts of ancient people. The later Apache and Yavapai arrivals were transient, hunter gatherers, and left little evidence behind other than potsherds, arrowheads, and manos and metates. The earlier dwellers were farmers who built pueblos of rock and left many items that the latecomers picked up and reused. In the archives at Sharlot Hall Museum in Prescott, Angie Mitchell's papers include a list of many artifacts she collected over the years, most of which were given to museums. She was doing this before current laws forbidding such collecting had come to pass.

On Saturday she and Mrs. Blake washed clothes, including Angie's soiled garments from the trip. She wrote, "Judge Blake went to Reno. The Prather Brothers have run the station there, but lately they have leased for a year to a man named…" She strikes a blank line in her diary, apparently not knowing his name.

"Reno" referred to Camp Reno, a military outpost of Fort McDowell from 1867 to 1870. Today the site, with a few ruins, can be accessed opposite Punkin Center in the foothills of Mt. Ord, a little over a mile from the Tonto Basin road (Highway 188). In 1880 Reno contained the local post office and had a store and a campsite for travelers. Isaac and William Prather, two bachelors who had come from Illinois, were 30 and 39 years old respectively and had kept the station at Reno.

That afternoon while the family had "gone across the creek after some stock" and Angie was alone, a frightening thing happened.

Chapter 5
The Move to Lower Tonto

The ranchers in Tonto Basin were about to receive their first schoolteacher. Angie Mitchell was staying at the Blake ranch on Rye Creek until the schoolhouse was prepared downstream on Tonto Creek, as well as a place for her to live. It was September 25, 1880, and the Blakes had gone to the store at Reno to get supplies and mail when Angie received an unexpected guest.

She wrote, "I had another surprise about noon. First, after I had changed my clothes, banged my hair afresh, and was wondering what upon earth I was going to do with myself the balance of the long, hot day, a stranger rode up. (He was) a rough, kindly looking miner. He viewed me with surprise and asked for Judge B(lake)."

At this point we wonder at her naivety. "He accepted my invitation to come in and wait, and suddenly turning said, `My little lady where on earth did a dainty bit of humanity like you drop from to light this dirty valley?'"

Her diary continues, "Who'd look for flattery of such broad description from such a source? I told him I had come to teach the Lower Tonto School, and would go there tomorrow. He stared and exclaimed, `*You* teach down there! It's like putting a hummingbird into a mud lark's nest.' "Angie added, "Now that's what I call encouraging."

She then proceeded to describe the outfit she was wearing. Her description gives us insight into the kind of clothing "city girls" were wearing in those days, but also the degree of vanity she was bringing to this rugged frontier life.

"I had on my pet dress for hot afternoons. A white lawn [1] with delicate pink flowers made with a ruffle edged milk-lace and beaded with the same; a broad sash tied at back of the lawn, tucked waist trimmed with insertion and lace and a little pink bow, cut pointed in neck and filled in with lace and rather short ruffled sleeves trimmed with more of the lace. All of ordinary quality and common style and not new, but clean and crisp. All my own make. My stockings were flesh color balbriggan [2] with pink Irido [3] on the instep and my slippers (I never wear shoes except when I must) one strap black opera sandals with bows. My skirts of course were all white and trimmed, and he may have seen the edges of them as I sat on the steps. But I haven't got a perfectly plain garment in my wardrobe and I wonder now if I had not better have made some."

As Angie's story unfolds her use of such detail, while tedious to some readers, will prove very helpful in picturing life as it was in frontier Arizona. While she was contemplating her attire, the Blakes returned. Angie heard the stranger say to them, "That's a dainty bit of girl-hood, but I'm sorry for her if she's to teach down yonder."

Then she heard Judge Blake respond, "She looks more like a living rosebud in that dress than anyone I ever saw. But she's got grit enough to teach any school around this country, and she'll run it to please herself."

Angie added, "Janie looked at me and laughed and said, `You'll need your grit in lots of ways.' …. Next time I go into barbarism I'll wear nothing but dark calico and unbleached sheeting, hot underclothes and hob nail shoes!" She learned that the miner's name was Louis Cordin. [4]

The next day, Sunday September 26th, Andy and Janie Blake take Angie to the ranch of John and Mary Vineyard where she would live until the teacher's house was built. Mary Elizabeth Vineyard was the sister of Narsisses Jane ("Janie") Blake, and both women were the daughters of David and Josephine Harer. Angie often refers to them as "the girls," and they became her closest support during her tenure in Tonto Basin. The Vineyard family included five children who would figure in Angie's diary: Willie - 10, Johnny - 9, Green - 4, Ezra and "baby Agnes." The first three were recorded in the 1880 census but somehow the last two were not listed there.

The diary follows the daylong trip to the Vineyard Ranch and on the way we are introduced to a number of Tonto Basin residents who will play prominent roles in the episodes to come. They pick up some of Angie's new students since many of the children of necessity live with the teacher or at the Vineyards' during the school term. The distances were too great for a daily commute.

"At Adams' Jeff Adams and Alice Crabtree joined us and went to Crabtrees' with us... At Tom Cline's we stopped for Belle Hook, and she came on home. We reached John Vineyard's about 5.... Mr. Harrer (sic) father to the `girls' was there also, and their younger sister Alice."

It needs to be understood that all of this takes place along Tonto Creek near today's Roosevelt Dam. Roosevelt Lake has covered the area since 1911. The Harer Ranch was a number of miles up Greenback Creek in Greenback Valley and their daughter Alice would live with Angie throughout her time there. Her reference to the Adams family is of interest because they had settled what later would become the 76 Ranch at the junction of Wild Rye and Tonto Creeks. John Quincy Adams and wife Emma settled there in 1877 and they had five children. John A. Adams was born in 1852; his twin brother Jack was called "Cap." [5] Jeff Adams, born in 1858, would later marry Alice Crabtree. Cordelia Adams, born in 1865, had married Bush Crawford in August, just before Angie arrived and they ranched at the mouth of Greenback Creek. A daughter named Texas Adams was born in 1868.

The Crabtree girl, Margaret Alice, was 14 or 15 years old and her family lived on the Lower Tonto. She had apparently been staying at the Adams' Ranch where her boyfriend Jeff Adams lived and now returned home with the party. Alice Crabtree's father and brothers were freighters, hauling supplies in and out of Tonto Basin.

She refers to Tom Cline. Thomas Jefferson Cline, born in 1852, was the son of one of Tonto Basin's patriarchal families, Christian and Margaret Cline. They had migrated from Indiana to California and after several other moves settled in Tonto Basin in 1876. Tom Cline married Leah Hook, daughter of James and Rebecca Hook, the year before Angie arrived. [6] Belle Hook, age 10, was at her sister Leah's and she joined the party as they made their way toward the school.

NOTES:

[1] A semi-sheer household linen.
[2] Balbriggen is a knitted, unbleached cotton fabric used for underwear. The name comes from a coastal town in Northern Ireland, probably the name of an ancient clan.
[3] Rainbow colors or iridescent.
[4] The 1880 federal census lists Louis Corden, 47 years old, from Apache County.
[5] His actual name was James Monroe Adams.
[6] Leah's name was actually Annie Leah Garner. Before her mother was married to James Hook, her previous husband was Leah's natural father.

Chapter 6
School Begins on the Lower Tonto

After five days living with Andy and Jane Blake on Wild Rye Creek they escorted teacher Angie Mitchell along Tonto Creek to the ranch of John and Mary Vineyard. There Angie would live until the ranchers finished building the teacher a house near the school. On the way there the little party picked up several of her students-to-be from other ranches. Several of the children would board with Angie and the Vineyards during the school term.

On her first day there the teacher used her ability for keen observation to provide us with a description of an 1880 ranch house in Tonto Basin. "September 26, (Sunday) The house consists of 1 room 16 by 16; dirt floor, pole house, thatched flat roof, no windows, open space; smak in the sides (calking between the logs). It has a rough fireplace and in this house live V. and his wife and 5 children: Will, John, Green, Ezra, and baby Agnes. Alice (Crabtree) and I are to stay temporarily. Great stars! It is located in a lovely place. Trees and fine views on all sides and nothing bleak or dreary about it.

"As to the furniture, 2 rough double bunks for bedsteads and hay-filled ticks – but four pillows, and that's luck! Clean, abundant homemade quilts, a long homemade dining table, uncertain on one leg; two or three boxes used as trunks pushed under the bunks; 6 or 7 homemade stools; a rough table; a fair cook stove and a fair collection of heavy white crockery, and quite a lot of tins. (There are) calico curtains around one bunk, a cracker box cradle, a small lamp, some more block or bottle candle sticks; a Bible, almanac, one or two stock books and a few old papers. And that's about all! Everything is clean and tidy though, and the family are very kind and pleasant spoken. V. is over six feet and built in proportion; while Mrs. V. is not much over 4 (feet) and weighs I guess about 90 pounds."

The next day, Monday, Janie Blake went home while her husband Andy remained to help his father-in-law, David Harer, finish the one-room school. The Greenback Valley settler was concerned that his grandchildren would have schooling and saw to it that the teacher was hired. David Harer also sponsored the building of the schoolhouse. [1] It would be the first schoolhouse in Tonto Basin and was located near the mouth of Greenback Creek.

The Harer family had migrated to Oregon in the 1850s. From there David's branch of the family moved to California, then on to Arizona. David and Josephine arrived in Tonto Basin in 1875 with their eight children and son-in-law Florence Packard. LeCount in his book *The History of Tonto* (page 68) writes, "At intervals some of the brothers of David lived on the Tonto, including Nathaniel Green Harer, a Methodist minister. He was a widower and his four children were reared by David and Josephine along with their own family." [2]

The schoolhouse was finished by nightfall that Monday, September 27th. It was about a quarter of a mile from the Vineyard house on the bank of Tonto

Creek. Tuesday morning school began with only four students. Andy Blake and David Harer returned to their homes while Angie wrote, "After school Alice (Crabtree) and I went to Mrs. Hooks', who is camped under a big tree." They probably were walking ten-year-old Belle Hook over to bid her mother goodbye. Mrs. Hook had camped there to see her daughter and son, 9 year old Charlie, through their first day of school. After she returned to her home, the children boarded with the Vineyards for the rest of the term. [3]

That night Angie wrote in her diary, "A man named Allison, alias Big Windy, stays at V's tonight. Evidently they keep a station too." Ranches in this isolated country often became "stations," places where travelers could refresh their horses and spend the night. The man, Allison, who spent that night there, does not appear in the 1880 census and is unknown to us. His nickname, "Big Windy," indicates he was a braggart.

On the second day of school, Wednesday, September 29th, Angie briefly records, "Johnny V. is a cripple so he has to ride and his mare is named Six Bits. Tonight while I was holding her and Alice saddling her, she bit us." Perhaps the mare's tendency to bite is the reason for her name, unless she was worth only $1.50.

The next two days there are no entries indicating the teacher was too busy with her preparations or too tired to write. However, she held classes on Saturday in order to make up for the previous Monday when the men were still building the schoolhouse. "The schoolhouse resembles V's abode, only it has no door and is not as high or as large."

Next we learn something of the 1880 Tonto Basin diet. "Oct. 3rd Sunday. Board consists of coffee, milk, bread, bacon, and dried apples, all well-cooked however. Twice we had beans and some jerky. Today it is bread and boiled chicken. Alice, Willie and I took a long, long walk. Got home at 7. A Mr. Persons has come to work for V. This house is like a New York omnibus!"

Although Angie was born on the east coast the Mitchell family moved to Kansas when she was about 4 years old. We assume she later visited New York to know what a "New York omnibus" was like. She probably means crowded and noisy. As to the hired hand, William Persons was a carpenter living in the Lower Tonto area.

On Monday as the school week begins, we meet the Armer children. "Oct. 4th, Sara and Melinda Armer aged 14 and 13 came to school this morning. They live over 7 miles from here on Salt River… Oct. 5th, Tom and Frank Armer came to school today." These boys were 10 and 8. [4]

The childrens' parents, Henry and Lucinda Armer, traveled throughout the western states before settling in Arizona at Grapevine Springs on the Salt River. It was about 6 miles southeast of the mouth of Tonto Creek. Their homestead became known as Armer Gulch and they lived there until the government purchased their land after the turn of the century because it would be covered by Roosevelt Lake. When they were required to move they established the A-Cross Ranch 4 miles north of Roosevelt on the road to Pleasant Valley.

NOTES:

[1] This information comes from Payson historians Jinx and Jayne Peace Pyle in correspondence with Stan Brown.

[2] Nearby the map indicates "Methodist Mountain," obviously named for or by the Methodist Harer family.

[3] The Hook children's older sister Leah had married Tom Cline.

[4] Melinda Armer would die while still a teenager. Tom Armer would become head of the family after their father died in 1909 and during World War I he was elected sheriff of Gila County. Frank never married and in the early 1920s he participated in a train robbery that landed him in the Territorial Prison at Yuma. He was shot during an attempt to escape and the resulting lung ailment caused his death the same year his father died, 1909.

Chapter 7
A Mountain Lion Tries to Get in

It was Angie Mitchell's second week teaching in the Tonto Basin School and she continued to live at the Vineyard ranch because the house being built as a "teacherage" was not yet ready. On Tuesday, October 5, 1880, she jots a very short and humble entry in her diary. "26 years old today. Tom and Frank Armer came to school today." We speculate that the Vineyards helped her celebrate if they knew about it and her unusually brief entry suggests she was tired and not in the mood to write.

On Wednesday, October 6th, she recorded a traumatic experience from the night before. "Last night I was wakened from sleep sometime after midnight by a tremendous purring noise. While wondering what it could be, I partly raised in bed and looked through a chink some 3 inches wide at the side of the bed, where a pole was taken out from the wall for ventilation. I was terribly frightened by having the mouth and nose of some animal thrust just opposite my face in an attempt to reach me. As I darted back with a scream, a big, furry paw stuck through the crack evidently trying to catch hold of me! I nearly fell out of bed over Alice in my anxiety to get out of the vicinity of that paw, and roused the family with my shrieks. These were echoed outside by a long, peculiar wail like a woman or child crying. Then I knew what it was for I've heard that wail many a time before. It was a cougar or mountain lion or

California lion. Vineyard had hung a small piece of beef up in the house close to the roof and on this same side, near a chink or two not as wide as the window over the bed. The lion has scented it and was trying to reach it when my move about attracted his attention and I presume angered him. The sound that awakened me was his purring, which I had never before heard one of them do. Peering cautiously out of a smaller crack, Alice and I could see in the clear moonlight three of them prowling around, a cub and probably the others were its parents. After watching awhile and being certain that no amount of clawing, even if he tried again, would admit the lion reaching me, I fell asleep again and the last sound I heard was one of the big cats climbing up the side of the house to the roof, probably thinking to reach the much desired beef from there."

They must have enjoyed telling the harrowing "lion story" Wednesday evening to a wayfarer, James Cook, who stayed the night. Angie writes, "This evening Jas Cook formerly Hartin's partner in the blacksmith shop at Ft. Whipple was here." Cook was 28 years old, a pack master with the army who was on his way from an assignment at Prescott's Ft. Whipple to Camp Bowie in the southern part of the territory. It must have been refreshing for Angie to receive some news from home. She knew Cook's former partner, John Hartin, who was a blacksmith in Prescott.

That same evening David Harer arrived bringing his 8 year old son, Asbury, and 12 year old daughter, Clara, to attend school and presumably to board with their married sister, Mary Elizabeth Vineyard. [1] He brought startling news with him. Angie records "the astonishing information that Janie Blake had a son who weighed after he was dressed barely 3 pounds, and was born the 4th inst.."[2]

Her diary entry continues, "As this event was not looked for until about Dec. 1st and she had made all her arrangements to go to Phoenix to stay with an old friend who was to nurse her, and expected to start this week so as to have time to make a wardrobe – why of course we were much surprised. The poor child did not have one single dud to wear, not even a diaper, and they rolled him up in an old quilt and went to the nearest neighbors a couple of miles away and borrowed some ancient baby duds. He was not weighed till after they returned with the clothes and dressed him."

Each day brought its surprises. On Thursday "Mary Vineyard (everyone speaks of everyone else in such a fashion here) [3] taught me to make mistletoe liniment; says it can't be surpassed for rheumatism and kindred ills." Then later that day the county superintendent of schools, William Hancock, arrived to inspect the new Tonto School. We recall that Hancock, when a soldier fighting the Apaches, had come upon and named Greenback Valley only later to meet the newly arrived Harer family in Phoenix and direct them to Tonto Basin and the lovely valley he had discovered. This visit from Hancock, who had become prominent in Maricopa County, was a happy reunion of old friends as well as an inspection tour. "He is very pleasant," records Angie, "but seemed greatly amused at my <u>stylish school house</u> [underline is hers] and I didn't blame him. He ate lunch with me at school. – bread, bacon and dried apple sauce – and we got quite well acquainted on school matters and on one another's opinions of how young ideas should be taught. He staid (sic) till 1 1/2 [o'clock] and then started to visit a school somewhere in the Globe District."

The young teacher was still waiting for her own place to live with the understanding that she would also harbor several of the itinerant children. David and Josephine Harer planned to come down from Greenback Valley to "repair an old dilapidated brush cabin and camp in it and board the school ma'am." However, the premature birth of the Harer's grandchild to Jane and Andy Blake held up progress. "This eve a note was sent down by Mrs. Harer saying that Janie was very low and the baby not likely to live, and asking as many of the Vineyard tribe as could… to come up."

Alice Harer and Willie Vineyard remained behind at Vineyard's with Angie to maintain the household and the school. "So we three and old Mr. Persons will run the ranch. Rained hard today." We assume it rained all day Friday and there is no entry that day but on Saturday the Harers and Vinyards, including the younger children, "started in the rain for Andy Blake's, 25 long miles."

After they left, the entry for Saturday continues with a sketch of everyday life. "Alice and I did up the dishes, cleaned up the house and then tackled a good sized washing. This afternoon we ironed all we could get dry between showers, and I baked some dried apple pies while Alice looked after the bread, which Mary `V' set last night. Mr. Persons killed and dressed some quail and we cooked those. This eve Persons brought home a small chunk of beef from Pemberton's."

NOTES:

[1] David Asbury Harer was born April 8, 1872, never married and died September 13, 1903. His name reflects the Methodist heritage of the Harer family.

[2] The use of the abbreviation "inst" was used in correspondence to indicate the present month and year. Janie Blake, we recall, was another daughter of David Harer, a sister to Mary Vineyard. The baby was named William Garfield Blake, born October 4, 1880.

[3] Angie is apparently getting used to informality on the frontier. In formal Prescott even husbands and wives were addressed as Mr. and Mrs.

Chapter 8
Life Settles in to Routine

Rain continued to fall in the Tonto Basin as the first week of October, 1880, moved into the second week. Sunday October 10, teacher Angie Mitchell writes, "It began to rain about sundown and fairly poured all night. Of course the house leaks and so we had a great time. This morning is bright, but Persons [the Vineyard's hired man] says the rain ruined Mr. V's barley. That will be too bad as it is about all they have and would be worth $200 or so."

That evening the Harer family members returned from Blake's up at the other end of the Basin where they had been helping with Janie Blake's new baby. Janie's sister, Mary Vineyard, remained behind and, anticipating their return, Angie had supper waiting for them. The next day, Monday, Alice (Vineyard) was "too ill to go to school and Six Bits [the Vineyard's horse] has run away so Johnnie, being lame, couldn't come to school. But Clara, Willie, Abbie, and the Armers were there." [1] By Tuesday Alice was better and school was "progressing nicely. A quieter, more obedient set I never saw."

The big event of the week occurred on Wednesday, when Mrs. Harer moved with Angie into "our new abode, about half way between Vineyard's and the `Tonto Academy.' We only had to go about one-half mile through the sand tonight instead of a mile as usual. Our `house' is primitive in the extreme and our furniture more so. But everything is clean, and I guess we'll get along O.K. Presently I'll get used to these ridiculous huts of mud and poles – or poles and weeds and mud as the case may be. Johnnie and Green [Vineyard] will stay here till Mrs. V. returns, so there are Mr. and Mrs. Harer, Alice, Clara, Abbie, Green, John and I." Then she adds this political note, "Hancock who is running for reelection spoke at Danforth's tonight and will speak at Cline's tomorrow night." [2]

Saturday, October 16th, was washday. Angie describes in detail the way Tonto Basin families washed their clothes in the creek. "Washed and ironed my belongings and it is quite a new way. We go to the creek bank, set a few rocks and build a fire; put a big zinc pail over it on the rocks and fill it with water. Then we take the one tub and put some water in it and soak the clothes. As we have at present no wash board, we hunt up a big rock, as nearly flat as possible, tote it to the edge of the water in the creek, and get another smooth round or oval one not very large. We take the clothes a piece at a time from the tub, put them on the big rock over which the creek flows, and soap them, then pound them well with the smaller rock. We keep them under the surface of the creek as long as we can. After we've hammered them we drop them into the zinc pail of hot water and cook them. Then we get another bucket, smaller, and a tin milk pan or two and rinse them and hang them out to dry on the sage brush and arrow weeds and various bushes.

"To my surprise my clothes look white and nice as if I'd had all the modern conveniences, and I washed over 80 pieces. There are two irons which we heat on the stove and I laid a long rather wide board on the dirt floor and put an old bedspread over it, and my ironing sheet over that. I knelt down on the spread and ironed on the board. It worked fine. We will have a table before next Saturday and ironing will be easier. Made Clara's doll a dress this eve… I finished the edging, crocheted, for the Blake's baby's skirt."

By the next day she reported "My shoulder which has been more or less lame since the rock episode on the 22nd is very much demoralized today. Probably I used an undue amount of muscular force when I hammered my wardrobe yesterday."

Then Angie adds a social note about some Tonto families. "Cap Adams and Mary Howard will be married this evening." Jack Adams is listed in public records as "Captain." His given name was James Monroe Adams and he married Mary Jane Howard October 17, 1880. She was 19 and he was 28. He died in 1899, she died in 1941 and they are buried in the Globe Cemetery.

Suddenly, the teacher's routine was about to be terribly upset. Janie Blake brought her new baby boy down to stay with her mother, Mrs. Harer, at Angie's "teacherage." The women along with Janie and the several children who boarded with the teacher "were eating breakfast when a great hullabaloo arose at the creek crossing just below our house, shouting and splashing of water etc. At first they thought it was a neighboring rancher driving a band of cattle across the creek, "when up to the house with a horrible whoop rode a band of Indians." What unfolded during the rest of that day was a horror story for the helpless women and children. This event undoubtedly concerned a band of Tonto Apache Indians. All of central Arizona's Native Americans had been confined on the White Mountain and San Carlos Reservations from 1875. At times small parties were given "passes" to leave the reservation to hunt wild game. At other times renegade bands broke from the reservation and conducted raids on ranches in the Tonto Basin area. These raids did not effectively end until after the Battle of Big Dry Wash in July 1882 when a band of 100 Apaches was defeated at East Clear Creek on the Mogollon Rim.

NOTES:

[1] Clara Belle Harer was born August 13, 1868, and died June 10, 1946. Her married name was Gish.

[2] Danforths lived in Richmond Basin on the way to Globe. In 1880 it was a ranching area, but by 1890 had become a silver mining camp. The Christian Cline family settled in Tonto Basin in 1886. Their sons John and Tom would marry into other Tonto Basin families.

Chapter 9
Attack by Apache Warriors

Three women, three children and a baby were eating breakfast Monday, October 18, 1880 and anticipating the beginning of a new week in the Tonto School. Mrs. Harer and three of her children, Alice, Clara and David (nicknamed Abbie), were still living with the teacher during the school year. Janie Blake and her newborn were there as well when "a great hullabaloo arose at the creek crossing just below our house, shouting and splashing of water."

At first they thought it was a neighbor moving his herd of cattle but suddenly "up to the house with a horrible whoop rode a band of Indians. The chief rode his horse into the house but when he found he could not sit erect on the animal after he got inside and could barely turn around on him, he dismounted, turned, walking all over Mrs. H's bed which was still on the floor and led him out. Then he returned followed by Indians till they quite filled the small room. We counted 14 and 1 half-grown boy. The bucks were in war paint and each had on a cartridge belt well filled, pistol in holster, a fine rifle in his hands, and all but one or two had big wicked looking knives. The boy had a knife and bow and arrows."

The band was undoubtedly Apaches from either the White Mountain or San Carlos Reservation where they had been confined since 1875. "We sat as if petrified thinking our time had certainly come when

Mrs. Harer (who is as brave a frontier woman as ever lived and is quite accustomed to the Indians as she has long lived near the San Carlos Reservation) arose, put on a brave face and stepping to the chief held out her hand with the customary `How!' The chief only gave a savage grunt and put his hand behind him."

Janie's baby was crying and the young mother got up and went to him taking up the attention of the visitors. In that moment, Alice slipped into the back room of the house and grabbed her little brother, Abbie, who had darted in there when the Indians first came in. The two children squeezed "through a narrow space near the kitchen chimney (and) fled, as I was certain, to John V's to warn them and get help if she could." The Vineyard's place was one half mile away from the teacher's house.

Angie continued her tale. "Mrs. H. asked where they were from, the conversation being mostly in Mexican which all the Indians of the country speak. He said they were Papagos. That was an awful lie for there's very little similarity between the Apache and Papago tribes. [1] Janie was trying to hush her baby and the chief glanced her way as if anxious to see the child. Usually the greatest mark of friendship one can show these savages is to exhibit their tiny and pink babies to them, and usually the Indians consider it an honor. So Janie, plucking up courage, moved a little nearer and unrolled the sheet and showed the chief what a tiny morsel he was. But (the chief) only frowned the fiercer and made a motion as if to seize the child and fling him down, but Janie clasped him closer and carried him to the farthest corner and deposited him. She then resumed her seat at the table near me, close by her baby and between the Indians and him. The chief and his band surveyed us in ominous silence, three lone defenseless women – one old, small and gray; one a slender girl, and the third, weak from recent confinement and now pale as death. Then after a few guttural sentences to each other, they seemed to decide on a plan. Grasping Mrs. H. firmly the chief held her hands behind her while one of the others tied them tightly with a buckskin thong. Then she was led to the opposite corner from us, placed in a chair and tied to the chair while a handkerchief laying handy was bound over her mouth. She struggled desperately but uselessly. During this performance Jane and I sat motionless. I could not have moved an eye lash, if by doing so I could have escaped what I believed to be the awful and certain death that awaited, for I was actually paralyzed by fright and I believe Janie was in a similar condition."

"I sat with my head a trifle drooping and my hands folded, pushed just a little back from the end of the table. One of the ugliest and most hideously painted of the Indians came and stood as nearly in front of me as my position permitted. Of course I did not look up at him. I couldn't, but putting his hand under my chin he jerked my head back with a force that nearly broke my neck. I looked at him then straight and unflinchingly in his cruel, gleaming eyes and I know I wondered if Satan in all his kingdom had a more fiendish looking devil. Something in my expression seemed to please him, the fear I could not hide probably, and with a wild whoop that made our nerves tingle (though neither Janie nor I jumped as one would suppose we would) he grabbed that great knife of his and grabbing me by my hair threw my head back as he drew his knife over my throat. But he did not touch it, that's sure or I wouldn't be writing this tonight. I think he must have touched my flesh with the back of the knife, for I am sure I felt the cold of the steel."

"I must have looked surprised when he dropped my head and I discovered it still rested securely on my shoulders. At any rate, another pleased look came into his eyes. Then he tore my sleeves open and pinched my arms and shoulders till I was blue-green and black most all over them. He slapped my cheeks, pulled my ears and pinched them, and then grabbed me by the bangs and pretended to scalp me. Not a sound did I utter all that time. I really believe if he had tied me to a stake and set fire to me I could not have even groaned. And I am sure would not have resisted."

"At last, as if tired, he paused a minute and glanced at Jane. Poor girl, she had submitted to the same torments only she wore earrings and the brute had torn one entirely down through her ear and the other nearly, and the blood was running freely from them. She like myself had not made a sound...."

NOTES

[1] The name Papago was given the tribe that straddles the Mexican border with Pima County, Arizona, and it is highly unlikely any of those people were in Tonto Basin. The word means "bean-eaters" but the tribe has gone back to using their original name - Tohono O'Odham or "Desert People."

Chapter 10
Escape From the Apaches

Tonto Basin teacher Angie Mitchell described the torture she and her companions were experiencing at the hands of a renegade band of Apaches. The day was Monday October 18, 1880, as her diary continues.

"At last my tormentor returned to his charge, wheeled the chair around and caused me to face the others. I saw that one Indian had my trunk open and he turned over some ribbons and things. I knew in a minute he'd reach my bundle of photos and a lot of little keepsakes, and that would be the last I'd see of them. Queer notion, to think of a trifling thing like that when I was positive that in an hour or whenever that fellow got done amusing himself, I'd be killed. But I'm not accountable for the vagary, and the thought put life into me and I sprang from my chair so suddenly that the buck did not have time to stop me if he had wanted to. I rushed to the Indian at the trunk who had just got a photo in his hand, grabbed it from him & dealt him a blow in the face so unexpected that he fairly staggered, flung the picture into the trunk, & the lid down, turned the key, & snapped the catches & put the key down my neck. The Indian whom I struck made a move as if to spring upon me but the chief said a word or two & he slunk back scowling.

"The buck to whom apparently the others had given me stepped forward, gave me a jerk & fling & sat me down so solidly that it took my breath, in the chair I had left. He stood & looked at me awhile & I felt again as if paralyzed & not able to stir. Then he, still regarding me closely, spoke to Jane's persecutor & they talked in Apache a little. Then my demon spoke to the chief, he in turn to the other Indians, & to my horror they all filed out, got on their horses, & rode off leaving those two with us. Then the one I seemed to belong to said something to the other & walked out.

"I sat still for there did not seem to be anything else to do. Suddenly Jane's possessor grasped me by the arm, jerked me out of the chair, & led me to the third & unoccupied corner of our brush house, stopped me about two feet from it & dropped my arm. I stood as he had left me - head a bit forward, arms by my sides, motionless. A rustle made me raise my head a bit and there within a foot of me & aimed squarely at my head was a Winchester rifle. As I gazed squarely at it I wondered that it had never before occurred to me what a big barrel those guns had. I heard the click of the trigger very closely - then, instead of finding myself dead, I was again grasped by Jane's Indian & dropped into my chair while <u>my</u> Indian, who had had the rifle at my head, came in & up to me & said, "Heap brave squaw. Mucho brave, mucho. Una pocita (that not spelled right, but it sounds like it) muchacha esta much brave." [Possibly *poseyo* from *poseer,* to control one's self, or self-control.] Such a funny mixture of Spanish & English! Then they turned to Jane and called her "mucho brave," "una bravisto mujer" & lots of such phrases. All meaning that they thought we were "brave" & they patted us on the shoulder & kept calling us "brave." At first I thought they were making game of us, but soon realized they were serious & really thought that it was courage that had prevented us from screaming or fainting or crying when they tormented us, and that while we had been so paralyzed with fear & terror as to be powerless to scream or even speak or to move hardly. Well! That's good!

"Mrs. Harer says she thinks the manner in which I sprang on that Indian at my trunk & made him leave it, went far toward causing them to think that if I wished to I could cry or scream or struggle, but then Jane & I were both acting on the principle that we would not give them the satisfaction of acting as though they hurt us. She also says that it was an inspiration that seized me to do that as the Apaches are great admirers of courage in anyone, particularly white women & that she believes we would have suffered much worse indignities if they had not been forced to respect our stoical courage. It looks to me like a silly piece of extreme idiocy on my part to think of trifles like that with death by torture staring me in the face, for not till they led me to the chair away from the gun did one gleam of hope dawn on me.

"Well, to return to my story, after praising us awhile they said to us (each of them addressing one of us) several rapid sentences in Spanish which I only half understood. But the little I did "sabe" turned me cold. Seeing, I suppose, that we did not comprehend all they said, they made a few rapid & unmistakable gestures and exhibited a certain portion of themselves to us that decency usually keeps covered. While we grew fairly frozen with an awful terror, they adjusted their garments again and led us to the doorway where my tormentor pointed to the sun, then towards the west, with this remark, `By maybe four o'clock, five o'clock come, we come.' He waited a minute & said it again more emphatically. 'Four o'clock come, we come.' I found my tongue & exclaimed, `The dickens you will. Well you won't find me here,' but they did not understand. Leading us back, they sat us down in our chairs & left the house, & in a minute were riding rapidly northward to the mountains nearby."

  The minute they realized they were alone the women sprang into action. As soon as Janie got up her strength gave out and she lost consciousness, falling to the floor. Mrs. Harer and Angie cut the thongs that bound her hands and were attempting to remove the handkerchief gag from Janie's mouth, when Angie also passed out.

  "Everything got black, & the rest is a blank as far as my personal knowledge goes for about half an hour... I found myself lying on Mrs. Harer's mattress with an odor of camphor-ammonia & H.H.H. [an unidentified herb] all about me & considerable dampness of hair & clothes. Mrs. Harer says that I remarked while at work on the knot of the handkerchief, `Poor Janie ill,' and then with some incoherent exclamation, fell to the floor like a dead person. She grabbed a butcher knife from the table, cut the handkerchief loose, dashed a pitcher of water over Jane. Then grabbed the bucket from the kitchen & treated me to its contents after which she got the camphor etc & treated us to alternate applications to our noses & rubbed camphor on our faces & slapped us vigorously & did everything else she could think of but without much success."

We recall that early in the episode Alice Harer had slipped into the back room of the pole house with her little brother and squeezed through a crack in the loosely constructed wall. She raced the half mile to the Vineyard ranch where she alerted Mary Vineyard and her children. They crept through the brush along the creek to get closer to Angie's house and then waited hidden until they observed the Indians leaving. When they were sure there were no more Apaches in the area they came out of hiding and entered the house. Seeing the two young women unconscious they thought them to be dead.

Angie continued her narrative. "(Mary's) mother reassured her as regards that and set her to work over us. Alice, whose hands were not numbed (as her mother's were by the cruel thongs), soon brought Janie to and a little while after, me. But when Jane & I tried to move, oh what torture. Our shoulders, arms, necks, heads, ears, & faces were so sore, & there were black & blue & discolored spots all around. Our hair had been pulled so hard as to pull our heads nearly loose, & we did feel as if it was impossible to move. The Apaches had come at 7 and left about quarter past ten. Unless we desired a worse fate to befall us that afternoon, we had much to do."

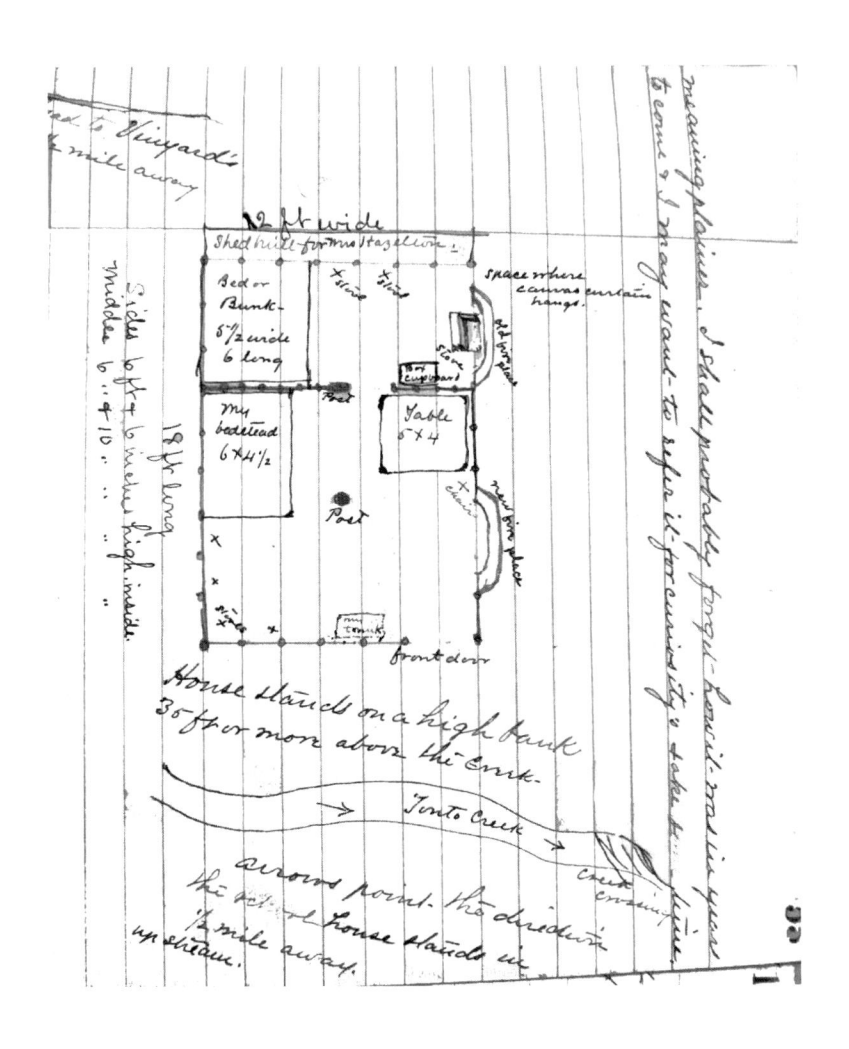

A page from Angie Mitchell's diary showing the layout of her house and its proximity to Tonto Creek.

THOROUGHLY SEASONED STOCK.   WILL STAND ANY CLIMATE.

SPRING WAGONS of all Styles but Only One Grade, that is the BEST.
Send for Catalogue and Prices.   Mention this paper.

Remains of Camp Reno — c. 1920

This is where mail was picked up by settlers.

David and Josephine Harer with David Jr.

62

General Crook Trail
   "13 Mile Rock".

Between mile markers 234-235.
This is near Government Mtn. where Angie camped the 1st night out of Camp Verde.

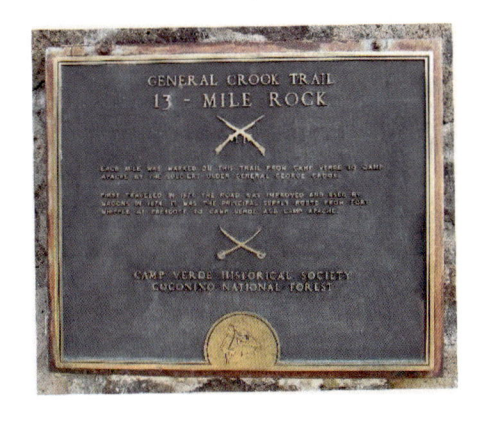

Mazatzal City Site

Pine Creek entering East Verde River just above center of photograph. This is where the Fuller family was ranching.

Doll Baby
Ranch Site

Tonto Creek

View of Tonto Creek looking downstream. It was along this river that Angie spent her months as a teacher.

A pole house under construction.

David H. Harer is David Asbury Harer, Sr.

Site of Camp Reno in 2013.

The spring at Camp Reno was part of the reason for its location.

Remains of Fort McDowell in 2013.

Captain Adna R. Chaffee who, with his wife, hosted Angie when she was on the way to catch the stage in Phoenix.

Tonto Creek as it was in Angie's time. This is the Wade family who settled in Payson.

Apaches, probably from San Carlos Reservation, and very like what Angie saw.

A view of what is now the Tonto National Monument c. 1920. This was closer to what Angie saw than it is today.

Final resting place of Angie and George—Greenwood Memory Lawn Cemetery, Phoenix, AZ.

Chapter 11
Cowboys Confront the Apaches

After a morning of harassing and torturing teacher Angie Mitchell and the other women, the renegade Apaches left with a promise to return at 4 o'clock that afternoon. Mary Vineyard and her children had been hiding nearby in the brush and seeing the warriors leave now made a stealthy approach to the teacher's house. They reported that "John Vineyard had gone off with 4 of the horses somewhere down the river to haul wood, but that a lot of men were mining over in the mountains some five or six miles & among us we could get them."

Angie's entries for October 18, 1880 continued. "We concluded to go to the mine where from 4 to 10 men worked, but for fear of missing them somebody had best ride to a camp of men collecting cattle about 5 miles away in another direction. And yet another (of us would ride) up to Hooks about 2 or 3 miles away to get him & his two hired men. We would not need all of them but time was precious & we probably would find some or all of them gone…

"Mary & the younger ones came up to our house while Clara, Alice, and Willie got up the three horses and Alice also caught an old buckskin pony that was grazing nearby, belonging to, none of us knew, or cared, who. The side saddle was put on for me, Mary's for Clara and Alice took a comfort & a cinch which she said was all she needed, while Will took Johnny's saddle. He thought he could find his father so started to try. Alice knew where the cattle camp was, or should be, & I could see the top of the mountain where the mine was, & so was least likely to get lost on that road of any of those roads we were to go, while Clara went to Hook's.

" The women figured the Apaches had returned to their hunting camp over the crest of a distant mountain. When Angie rode past the school, one half mile from her house, she found two of the Armer children wondering why there was no school. She sent them on home, explaining there would be no school the next day either. The teacher then crossed Tonto Creek and headed for the mine. There she found just two men who told her the others had gone to Phoenix. "They were very kind & I explained that perhaps their ride would be after all unnecessary as the cattle men & the balance might be at home, but they came just the same, & brought guns & ammunition. They made me rest about ½ an hour & gave me some strong hot coffee that helped strengthen me. We got back at 3 1/2 and found that Clara had returned an hour or more before without any of those she went for as she could not find them. 15 minutes later riding fast came Alice & 7 of the cattle men, armed & anxious for a chance to clean out the Apaches."

Soon after this John Vineyard and a friend arrived from their wood gathering, making eleven "able bodied men. Two of the men were elected to remain at the house to protect the women, while the other nine went after the Apaches. No sooner had the cowboys left, than the two Indians who had taunted the women the most came riding up. True to their promise of returning about four in the afternoon, they dismounted and walked boldly into the house.

"They entered the room & looked astonished to see two stout fellows covering them with rifles. (They immediately said), `Don't shoot, don't shoot - me go,' and started, but the cowboy slid between them & the door with the remark, `No you don't till you tell what you are doing here, you sneaking, red skinned etc.'

"They said they were White Mountain Apaches on a hunt, that they were two parties with squaws and that they met about 8 or 10 miles from here, left the squaws in camp and came on to hunt in the mountains beyond us. That they stumbled on this house by accident and they were only in fun; didn't mean to hurt us any, only to scare us and one of them said, `Heap brave squaws no scare, so we try to make scare, but she no scare.'"

One of them had a pass from the San Carlos Agency, and it was illegal to kill an Apache who was there on a pass, unless for self-defense. "So the cowboy had to let them go, first promising what he and the rest would do if they ever came near us again. He told them to `Vamos' & they left in a hurry."

Two hours later the other men returned, reporting the Apaches they encountered also had passes, and that "the chief said his men were just in fun. It was impressed on them that any more such fun in that vicinity would be very costly to them & they were ordered to get out of those mountains and not return, but go farther away or they would wish they had."

The Vineyard family and one of the cowboys stayed at the teacher's house all night. That evening Angie wrote her diary entry with much effort. "I can scarcely write for my lame arm and shoulders and Janie is too ill to sit up, but the baby is as fine as a fiddle & very quiet. Mrs. Harer is all stiffened up from her enforced sitting in one position for 3 hours or more, and her wrists are very painful. It puzzles us all why the fiends did not kill us. Mrs. Harer's theory is that they saw four of us, Alice, Janie, Mrs. H. & I when they first came, that they knew there was but one doorway to the house and as they guarded that did not think of anyone getting away. So as Alice escaped like `a streak of lightening' while their attention was engrossed for a moment by Janie and her baby, they did not miss her for awhile, Jane and I were too much occupied with ourselves and the two who teased us to pay a great deal of attention to the movements of the other Indians, but Mrs. Harer, securely tied in the corner, closely watched all their actions. She had not missed Alice herself at first, but when she did she knew Alice had gone to V's (whose house by the by is completely hidden around a bend in the road and behind a hill from this place)."

Angie continues quoting Mrs. Harer's observation of how the intruders discovered one of the girls missing. "The Apaches talked a little to each other, she says, and pointed to us and to her and then to the other room and one of them went into the room and returned saying something, upon which several of them went out and were gone some little time. When they came back they said several sentences to the chief who scowled worse than ever. She says her opinion is that they missed Alice suddenly and went to the other room and found her gone; trailed her to the road till they came to Vineyard's. Willie and Clara say there were several moccasin tracks near the house. The Indians found the house deserted and realized that someone had undoubtedly gone for help, perhaps sent a courier to Ft. McDowell about a day's ride away. They knew the girl could give information against them, and their numbers were too few to hope to make a success of an extended raid. The safety of themselves and their squaws (we afterward learned they were camped 8 or 10 miles away at a spring) depended on changing their original intentions and becoming a peaceful party of hunters out on passes. This accounts also for the fact that they were in war paint, and hideous it was when they came in the morning. But they had no paint on when the men saw them in the afternoon. Not even the two who returned to our cabin. Their original plan when they left the squaws was probably to rush thru the lower Tonto country and kill all defenseless people and destroy isolated places where they could. Then after a few days of this sort of amusement return to the squaws, divide into smaller parties and get back to the reservation from an opposite direction and disclaim all knowledge of any raid, leaving it to be supposed that the crimes were committed by some small renegade band. But Alice's lucky escape caused them to change their plans. Likely they did not know that there was another ranch so near us until they trailed her to it."

After Mrs. Harer gave her assessment, with which everyone agreed, they were relieved and happy to believe that Alice's escape had saved their lives. However, it remained a mystery as to why the two tormenters returned in the afternoon if the Apaches' plans had changed as Mrs. Harer suggested.

Chapter 12
Skunks and Cattle Stampedes

The day after teacher Angie Mitchell's torturous day with the Apache warriors she wrote (Tuesday October 19, 1880), "Too lame to more than scrawl a line. Jane in bed. Mrs. Harer came tonight and was greatly surprised to find a lot of semi-invalids done up in liniment, salve and arnica." Arnica is a liquid preparation made from the dried, yellow-orange flower heads of the perennial herb "Arnica Montana." Similar looking to daises, this plant originated in Europe and since the Middle Ages has been used to treat bruises and sprains.

By the next day she was able to teach school though her arms were still very sore and she held an extra class on Saturday to make up for Monday's absence. Each night during that week she got little sleep because Jane's new baby, who was sick, kept everyone wakeful with constant crying.

On Sunday "a big skunk came in and made things rattle at a lively rate for awhile but Mrs. H. got after him and he left." The next night the creature returned creating even more excitement. Angie wrote on Monday, "My goodness but this is a lively place to live, only a bit wearing on one's nerves. Last night at Mrs. H's request I `exhumed' my 42 caliber pistol from the bottom of my trunk and laid it handy when we retired about 9. Baby cried steadily till 12, then grew quiet and everyone went to sleep. About 1 o'clock a skunk got in and Mrs. Harer sprang up, called me as she ran outside after the skunk. I grabbed that gun of mine and followed barefooted, and got a fair shot at the skunk. It tumbled him over, but in a second he jumped and ran into a cat claw bush. Mrs. Harer seized a pole from the woodpile and beat round till she dislodged him and he broke for another bush. She followed, striking violent blows at him without however damaging anything but the ground. Meanwhile Jane and Alice had put a board about two feet high across the door and stuck two stools against it to prevent his coming back into the house. I, out in the sand, rocks and brush, had concluded that bare feet were not best calculated to run around on..."

Angie turned to return to the house and get her slippers, but unaware of the barricade the girls had put in place the teacher tripped over the board, "fell over it and onto it and through it and ricocheted wildly around with those stools till I finally landed in a heap under the table at the other side of the room. (I had) several abrasions on my limbs and the more prominent parts of my anatomy, uncertain whether it was myself or some other person, and not quite clear as to what had happened to me for the room was dark..."

As Angie came to her senses the baby "was yelling at the top of his lungs" and Mrs. Harer was calling loudly for them to come outside. Alice ran out ahead of Angie only to receive an unintended blow on the head from Mrs. Harer's wild swing of the stick against the skunk. The teacher followed just in time to see this happen and reported, "I decided that in this case discretion was the better part of valor and fell into the rear of the procession. His skunkship crawled into a sage brush and then Mrs. H., Alice and I demolished him with poles."

Retreating to the house they changed their clothes as they had received "a liberal dose of perfume." Although it had become very cold outside they carried their soiled clothes to the creek, along with soap and towels, and all plunged into Tonto Creek. They got rid of the smell as best they could, put on their clean nightgowns and "carried the old ones on sticks a little way down the creek and buried them in the sand. Then we went back to bed."

The Blake baby was worse the next day, Monday, and they sent a cowboy after the baby's father, Andy Blake, "who is coming home from Phoenix and must be somewhere on Reno mountain by now…" However that night she would report regarding the baby, "Worse and more of it."

The Hook family was in the process of moving and spent the night with the teacher. "Mrs. Hook slept with me and she snored and snorted so, and tossed around like a restless child. My sleep was of short duration. While I was meditating about sliding out on the floor with a quilt, there arose a great barking of coyotes and bellowing of cattle some ways up the mountain side above us. It awakened us all and in a minute we heard the hoof beats of the panic stricken cattle and their bellowing grew nearer. We sprang out of bed and rushed in a body for the door, sure that the stampeding herd would rush straight though our frail house and probably crush us as well. Everyone grabbed the first thing they could that would aid in frightening them. Alice and I were first out and each had a sheet, so we ran round to the side the cattle were coming from and faced them. Not more than a hundred yards away, tearing along on that manner peculiar to a badly frightened hare, and making straight for our house in their mad rush for the creek and safety, were about 100 head of stock. We took a firm hold of our sheets, flapped them up and down and ran forward yelling as loud as we could. Directly behind came Mrs. Harer and Mrs. Hook, each beating a tin pan with a stick and yelling, and behind them Clara and Belle with an old tin can and a spoon for Belle and a big white apron and old tin horn of Abbie's for Clara. Each was swelling the noise as well as they could and Clara wildly waving her apron in one hand.

"Such an awful powwow was too much for the cattle and they swerved, passed each side of us and our house so close they nearly grazed us and went on tearing through the bushes and rushed across the creek. We returned out of breath and badly scared to find poor Janie just lying outside the door in a faint with her baby wrapped in a blanket close to her. We brought her to and took care of the baby, built a little fire and got hot water to make tea for Jane. At last we subsided into our peaceful beds."

The next morning the spirited team found that the cattle had demolished the brush arbor they had erected by the creek for shelter when they washed their clothes. Their tub, wash bucket, bench and stool had been smashed to pieces, and several items of clothing that had been left to dry on a clump of bushes were trampled or had been "carried in fragments away on their horns."

Two nights later, lions screaming in the distance set off the cattle herd and another stampede ensued. This time the herd was not as large and the women took their implements and waved off the cattle farther from the house. "A few more nights of this sort of business and we'll all be crazy."

Chapter 13
A Typical Weekend in Tonto Basin

After the excitement of the Apache attack and the cattle stampedes, life for the teacher and her students' families returned to mundane events. On Thursday evening "David's (Harer) oldest brother arrived unexpectedly from Oregon and says a lot more of their relatives will be here in a few days." The next day, on Friday, October 29th, the teacher's small house was quite full. Angie writes, "We're thick here this evening. David Harer and wife, Blake and wife and baby, James Harer, Alice, Clara, Abbie and myself in this tiny house."

On Saturday morning Angie took Alice for the 20 mile trip to "old Camp Reno" where they would pick up the mail and purchase needed items. She was driving a buckboard wagon owned by James Harer and pulled by a team including one of Vineyard's horses and a mule belonging to the Hook family. It was a good instance of the several families all working together for survival in this out of the way place. "Cline's old billy goat followed us to Reno." They got to the trading post at 1:20 in the afternoon, stayed an hour, and then began the trek home. However, it was dark when they reached the Crabtree's Tonto Basin ranch and since "some bad creek crossings" lay ahead they decided to stay overnight.

Her entry for Sunday, October 31 records her trip home and the fact that they "brought Mattie Crabtree home with us to go to school this week…" Mattie is

Margaret Alice Crabtree. "I brought home from Reno for the folks some candles, coffee, sugar, combs and several other needfuls. Haven't had either coffee, sugar or tea for a week except a little tea that we saved for Jane and the combs have all been missing since the Indians visit, and perhaps they took them tho' what for I cannot guess, for I don't believe they ever use one."

Upon reaching home she discovered that during her absence Mrs. Harer had an accident chopping wood. A "stick flew up and hit her on the nose and upper lip and blackened her eye. Her nose bled profusely and today it and her lip are swelled to three times their usual size and her eye is nearly closed and black and blue around it. She looks like a prize fighter in petticoats…Mrs. Harer presents an amusing appearance though we are all sorry for her."

That afternoon the community gathered for Sunday worship at Angie's house. She writes, "Mr. James Harer (who is an old preacher) delivered a very good sermon today at our house to an audience of 21 people. But I regret today that I had extreme difficulty in repressing a smile at his appearance. His beard and hair are rather long and very gray, but nicely combed, and he has one very sore foot, caused by some accident enroute from Oregon. He cannot wear a boot, so he, like `my son John' in the fable of the stockings, had `one boot off and one boot on.' He wore a dark calico shirt rather short as to sleeves, and a pair of overalls, and wore no coat. His queer costume was about all I could think of."

The "old preacher" James Harer may be the senior

Harer, father of David and born in 1818 according to an 1880 census. One of his sons was also a Methodist minister. LeCount in his *History of Tonto* (page 68) writes, "At intervals some of the brothers of David lived on the Tonto, including Nathaniel Green Harer, a Methodist minister. He was a widower and his four children were reared by David and Josephine along with their own family." After the service Angie took six of her students and "went over and dug into some old Aztec graves and got several specimens of carved bone, ornaments, beads etc." She reflects the common opinion of settlers that the prehistoric ruins and artifacts throughout Tonto Basin were left by Aztec people from Mexico.

    On Tuesday, November 2 Angie refers in passing to "election day today," without any details. It would be interesting to look at the politics of Tonto Basin folks those days though she does not speak of such. The presidential election that year was held up in the Electoral College until finally James A. Garfield was elected as a compromise candidate. He took office the following March but served only until July 2, 1881, when he was assassinated.

    The week passed without incident until Thursday night when another encounter occurred with Mr. Skunk. The frequent invasions of critters must be attributed to the loose construction of the pole houses in the basin like the one the Harers built for Angie. She writes, "Thursday Nov. 4, More excitement last night. Alice, Mrs. H. and I retired about 10. Mattie, Belle and

Clara were asleep much earlier in the back room. About 12, I who was sleeping uncommonly sound, was awakened by something warm and moist licking the little finger and the one next to it on my hand, which hung down on the side of the bed. I drew it up with a jerk and raised, and looked down on the floor and beheld a pretty little spotted skunk – nothing more nor less than one of the dreaded `hydrophobia cats' of Arizona. My, but did I scream. Mrs. H. sprang up barefooted on the floor in the other part of the room, but I told her to look out for we had a little skunk in the house. Then striking a light before she crossed the room, she saw the skunk sitting close to the head of my bed with our chicken beside it, dead. The chicken had been roosting in an uncovered box under the bed. She threw me my shawl, into which I scrambled quickly and got out at the foot of the bed. We each got a long stick and standing at a respectful distance we urged his departure. He took the hint and moved to the door, stopped every second or two to face us and pat, the way they move their forefeet on the ground when angry. Finally, we got him outside and we had the good luck to kill him, but our chicken was useless to us now so we flung it away too. The younger ones had watched this performance from the safe shelter of their beds."

"No Arizonan attacks a `hydrophobic cat' unless it is necessary, for their bite is almost certain death. It is not long since two men living up the creek away, died in the terrible agonies of hydrophobia induced by the bite of one of these pretty looking little animals under circumstances similar to ours. We examined my finger and found it was not bitten. He had only lapped it kitten fashion and wasn't I grateful."

Chapter 14
An Invasion of Harer Family Members

    It was Thursday, November 14, 1880 when Tonto School teacher Angie Mitchell met the extended family of David and Josephine Harer and found there were more of them than she had realized.

    The "great migration" of Harer family members began in the 1850s with a westward trek from Lawrence County, Arkansas, to California. Evan and Obedience (McClendon) Harer brought at least four grown children and numerous grandchildren. They were David Asbury Harer, Obedience Hazelton, Nathaniel Green Harer, and Redman Harer along with their spouses and children. By 1870 they had settled in as farmers in Santa Barbara County. [1] But in 1875 the restless nature of the pioneer mind got the better of David A. Harer. He and Josephine moved their eight children to Arizona sojourning in the fledgling town of Phoenix. As noted earlier, there they encountered Phoenix Postmaster William Hancock who, as a cavalry officer, had located and named Greenback Valley in the Sierra Ancha. He shared with them the virtues of this still virgin valley along a flowing creek that found its way down to the Tonto. It did not take much persuasion for the land-hungry Harers to cross the Mazatzal Mountains and stake their claim to Greenback Valley.

    Angie wrote in her diary, "This evening at 8:30 our family received quite an occasion. Mrs. Obedience

(Beady) Hazelton, two sons, three daughters, and Newton Green Nathaniel Harer with two sons and two daughters arrived. [2] They are relatives from Oregon who were expected next week. Mrs. Hazelton is Mr. Harer's only sister and Mr. Green Harer is a younger brother of David, and is a widower, while Mrs. Hazelton is a widow." [3] Angie goes on to list the names of 18 Harer grandchildren, all of whom she would have in her school. It is no wonder David A. Harer planned to build a school and hire a teacher for his brood. Furthermore, it is little wonder that the teacher in listing everyone gets somewhat confused as to names and who belongs to whom. Many of these children would grow and marry into Tonto Basin families, accounting for practically the entire population of the area in the late 19th century. For example, the eight children of David and Josephine Harer were as follows.

    Mary Elizabeth, born in 1832, married John Vineyard in 1867 while they were still in California and by the time Angie came to Tonto they had five children. Six more would be born after 1880. There had been a second daughter, Evaline, born in 1855 who apparently died at birth. Annie Eliza Harer married Henrich Frederick Christian Hardt in 1875 and they would have eight children.

    Narsissis Jane Harer, "Janie," married Andrew Blake in January before Angie arrived on the scene. Her baby boy had been quite sick and her mother Josephine was helping to care for him when the Apache Indians attacked them. (See previous chapters.) Janie and Andrew had two other children in the next few years. It is sad to note that in January of 1887, at age 28, Janie committed suicide, though a mystery surrounds her death. An undated newspaper clipping in the Sharlot Hall Museum at Prescott, from *The Tempe News*, states, "A Mrs. Andrew Blake of Tonto Basin has committed suicide by shooting herself." However, a more recent comment by a genealogist states, "Narsissis Jane Harer Blake was shot and killed by her second husband, Andrew Blake at Greenback, Gila County, AZ."

Sarah Frances Lincoln Harer was born on January 25, 1861 and in 1876 at the age of 15 she married Florence Packard. Over the following 24 years they had 12 children. Because of her middle name, she was given the nickname of "Linky."

Alice Lurinda Harer was born May 30, 1865. She married Edward Charles Conway in January 1888 and they had six children. Clara Belle Harer was born August 13, 1868. She married several times and in 1895 married Pascal Augustua Lindsay. They resided in Globe, Arizona.

The youngest of David Asbury and Josephine Harer's children was born April 8, 1872 and named after his father. His nickname, often used in Angie's diary, was "Abbie."The name "Asbury" reflects the Methodist heritage of the Harer family. Asbury, England is dear to Methodist hearts having played an important role in the life of founder John Wesley. A mountain not far from Greenback Valley is called "Methodist Mountain" after this family. In her diary, Angie expanded on his name saying the full name was David Corwin Asbury Gleason Reeder Harer. This does not show in any census records and must have been family talk she picked up from Mrs. Harer. In any case, the name Gleason Asbury Reeder is further evidence of the Harer's Methodist connections. The Rev. G. A. Reeder was a Methodist missionary from the midwest sent to Arizona where he was influential in establishing the first churches in the territory.

    The teacher's diary for this day of the great influx continued, "Such another time as we've had getting settled for tonight. Green and the three older boys slept in the wagon. Mrs. Hazelton with Mrs. Harer and Regie and Mary; Sarah, Alice, and I together; Laura and Ida on one pallet and Belle and Clara on another and we made a bed for little Abbie on the table, and tucked Francis crosswise in Ida's bed."

    Friday, November 5th was her first day to teach that large assemblage of cousins. "Such a day. I foresee that I shall have plenty of trouble with George Hazelton who is his mother's darling and as ill-conditioned a young cub as I've ever seen. Frances and May and Georgie have been staying at the Hazelton's since their mother died and the boys, particularly George, have evidently run rough shod over them. Georgie and May cry at everything while Francis pouts. [4] Laura, Belle and I slept together tonight. Alice being at Vineyard's and Laura insisting that the floor hurt her back, which is a little lame, so Sarah who is not lame offered to exchange and of course I'm satisfied with any of them. The place resembles chaos."

Angie had planned to have a make-up session of school on Saturday but the fathers wanted use of the school in order to build more seats for the growing attendance. As it turned out there was a lack of lumber and the building project was put on hold. "So the children and I put in the day exploring old ruins. Mrs. Harer kindly stole out my washing and did it this week for me – greatly to my surprise. And so I am free to do as I please. "

On Sunday, November 7th "Belle and Clara went to Crabtree's for an Indian (Aztec) bowl Mrs. Crabtree found in the big ruin and gave to me, and broke it in 20 pieces." The children must have dropped it on the way but their teacher is very reserved and does not chastise them. Exploring old ruins is one of Angie's favorite hobbies. This is reflected in her earlier diary from Prescott and here in Tonto Basin she discovered a bonanza of artifacts to collect. As far as we can tell she never sold these items but most of them ended up in local museums.

She lived like a true pioneer woman without complaint about the hardships and apparently taking the primitive conditions in stride even though she had come from an educated and sophisticated background. She does not expect to be waited upon and babied but fits in with whatever each day demands. It is no wonder the people of Tonto came to love and appreciate her.

NOTES:

[1] The family name is usually spelled with two "r"s in the Federal Census records. By the time they reached Tonto Basin the spelling Harer was more common though Angie vacillates between the two spellings in her diary.

[2] The teacher is a bit confused here if the census records are correct. Obedience Hazelton had three sons and two daughters: Carter (whom Angie had not met at this point), Ida, Laura, George, and Charles.

[3] Another branch of the family, a nephew of David A. Harer also named David, had settled with his family at Goose Lake, California, a lake that straddles the California Oregon border. Angie may have heard stories of the family's early entry to Oregon before migrating to California, and here she confuses the facts.

[4] The father of these three children was Nathaniel Green Harer, who had arrived with the others as a widower.

Chapter 15
How to Build a Pole House

By the first week of November, 1880 Angie had 23 pupils squeezed into a structure that was ten by twelve feet, dirt floor, no door, and sides made of brush. There were seats for only 12 students and how the others were able to do their work she did not say. Suddenly she remembers "that I have never described the style of architecture adopted for 'our' mansion - so I'll do it now."

In a lengthy diary passage she provides a detailed description of the "pole house" the Tonto Basin families built for their teacher and a number of her students. This ancient form of construction seems to have been popular in the early days of Tonto Basin settlement. They were not only quite sturdy, they were made of materials at hand and the cost lay primarily in the manual labor. Since this construction in the early settlements was popular it is worth allowing teacher Angie Mitchell to record for posterity the building process.

"A space is cleared on the ground from brush, and leveled. Then poles, mesquite in this case, about as large as a medium size fence post, and 8 ½ feet long, are set into the ground for a depth of 2 feet. The poles on two sides and one end are two feet apart, but on one end a space of nearly 4 ft is left and, again, the rest of that end has poles 2 ft apart. The bark is always peeled off of all the posts and poles.

"Another pole of the length of the house (or perhaps 2 poles are required to make the desired length) smaller around than those set in the ground, is fastened on top of the row of poles. This is repeated till the four sides are made. Then two big posts are set at equal distances from those forming the ends, midway between the sides and it looks from above about like this." At this point she draws a rectangle with two dots for posts, one in each half.

"Our house is 14 feet wide by 18 feet long. Then a row of poles about a foot apart is set for a partition between the rooms and covered with slips of canvas, leaving a door 2 ½ feet wide near the middle of the partition. The two rooms thus formed are respectively 14x12 and 12x6.

"Now across the top poles are laid, stout ones extending from the end of the house to the middle posts. These middle posts are 10 inches through and are cut so as to leave a crotch at the top. [She draws a "Y"] In this house there are two such ridge poles. The middle posts are 4 inches higher than those at the sides, which since they were set 2 ft in the ground are only 6 ½ feet high.

"Next smaller poles 3 or 4 inches through are nailed from the ridge pole to side poles - 2 ft apart. Then brush and yucca plant leaves and tules are usually woven thro and secured. In our case they are only lain (sic) on top of the poles and fastened. Then mud, the regular adobe clay kind, is plastered several inches thick over the outside of the tule on the roof.

"The next thing is to fill in the 2 ft. spaces at the sides and ends. This is done by weaving masses of arrow weed thru them till they are thick enough to suit. Wherever a window is desired a space is left open. The floor is dirt & kept `walkable' by frequent sprinkling & brushing. We have no door & no window curtains."

Having pictured the basic construction, Angie now turns her description to the interior of the house.

"A chimney is built in our parlor with a fireplace of rough rocks laid up in mud. In our kitchen is a similar fireplace which is all tumbled down except the fireplace part. Mrs. Harer has set her No 7 stove, and the pipe extends up 3 joints, then has an elbow and joint, and is secured by wires extending to the roof. On the side is a space that is a foot wide or more, close to the fireplace, where she has fastened a kind of canvas curtain. This is always up in the daytime to admit air and light. It was through there that Alice made her escape when the Indians came.

"Our furniture consists of a bed stead which extends across the end of the `kitchen' (6 ft) and is 5 1/4 ft wide, coming within inches of the doorway between the rooms. The bed stead is made of rough brushes, with a solid bottom in place of slats. A stool and the stove are all the furniture there except 3 boxes of clothes under the bed. The bed itself is of loose hay with a piece of canvas thrown over it and tucked in around it, with plenty of quilts and good pillows."

"Our parlor has a table 5 ft. long & 4 wide (for our dining) and a table which stands in the corner. It extends close to the door, opposite is my bed and anyone who sleeps with me. Mrs. H. explained in the beginning that *that* was the `school ma'ms' bed and she desired it distinctively understood that whomever I chose for my `room mate' was my own affair. As the bed is big and I am satisfied with any of them, it has been easy to adjust matters satisfactorily to us all. This bed is left long and is 4 ½ feet wide. It has a good straw bed, and a husk mattress on top of it and has slats, lots of quilts, and a pair of nice soft pillows. My trunk stands nearby. Mrs. H. makes her bed down at the foot of mine sometimes, but lately has put it over by the table opposite, and close to the fireplace. There are 6 home-made stools and 1 chair, and a kind of box cupboard is in the kitchen which I forgot to mention, which holds our dishes. Nails are driven up in the side poles at intervals and we hang our clothes on them. That's all except a little tin ware, a skillet, baking pan or two, box on which the flour sack sets and cans for sugar, coffee and tea etc. There is a ft. square looking glass which somebody cracked the other day and now it gives the one brave enough to look in it the appearance of having their face split in the middle lengthwise, one side an inch higher than the other. It is ugly enough to give a person a fit!

"There's a rough shelf over the fireplace made by driving pieces of a broken ramrod into the mud between the stones at the ends. And a hewn, wedge shaped stick in the middle, flat on the top is driven in the same way. Placing a clean rough board 10 inches wide on these supports forms the mantel.

"We have had two tablecloths but one disappeared with my skirt & Alice's drawers and Clara's chemise the night of the stampede, so we've only one."

The teacher now provides some insight into their diet.

"Mrs. Harer is a good cook but has little to do with. We have however good solid grub and lots of it and could eat six meals a day if we wished for all she would care. Our usual fare is coffee strong & clear, hot biscuit, bacon, gravy or stewed jerky, molasses (not syrup) and potatoes in some shape for breakfast, with milk one of the children gets from Vineyard's. For dinners to carry to school she loads our bucket with bread or biscuit, some with molasses on, some without, cookies or molasses cake, which is always light and nice, sauce of dried apples or peaches and a huge bottle of milk. Supper is tea, cold loaf bread - salt rising - cake or cookies or pie of dried fruit or sauce. Beans sometimes, cabbage sometimes, gravy of some sort and potatoes always. Once in a while cooked onions. Occasionally she has been able to get a small piece of beef, and three or four times chickens. But she has neither eggs or butter. Now that is much plainer living than most of our country folks in Yavapai have, but it is always so well cooked and so neatly served that it is ample and I don't care for more variety. I don't eat bacon, nor beans and rarely care for dried apples in any form, but I wouldn't tell her I never eat them for anything."

Chapter 16
A Gila Monster Comes to School

The young teacher at Tonto School was about to encounter another unwelcome critter, this time in her classroom. It was Friday, November 12, 1880, a warm summer day according to her diary.

"I furnished a good deal of amusement for my school today quite unexpectedly. I was hearing a geography class and feeling something tugging at my dress as if there was a weight on it, shook it off and went on with my class. Presently feeling it again I looked down and there lying on my dress skirt, in array of sunlight, was as hideous a reptile as I've ever seen. He was black and yellow and tawny, and had a body like a monstrous lizard, a spiky-looking tail, and a head like a snake. It was over a foot long.

"Lord! I gathered up my dress, and with a yell one could hear a mile, jumped on the stool I had been sitting on."

She goes on to report that "the commotion that ensued beggars description." Several of the female students upon seeing the monster followed their teacher's example and jumped up on the furniture. The youngest child broke out in frightened sobs. However, some of the older children who had seen these creatures before laughed and said, "Why teacher, that's nothing but a Gila monster."

"Well. I've heard lots of stories about those uncanny dwellers in Arizona." Angie continued, "but

I've never seen one before, at least on his native heath. I was sufficiently reassured to collect my wits, but I took pains to jump off my stool on the side the monster was not."

She called for a recess and while the children went out to play she invited more information from the experienced ones. "The scholars said that by some the Gilas were believed to be poisonous, but that they personally knew that some people actually petted them, and that they did not bite unless very angry. It was not an easy matter to make one angry enough for that, but they could blow themselves up, as Willie phrased it, `and puff their breath in your face and make you awful sick.'

"In the meantime our Gila has leisurely taken himself home and disappeared down a hole in the corner near my desk."

After this the "monster" became a regular visitor in the classroom and the teacher sought to befriend it. On Thursday, December 2nd she recounts what happened during the interim of several weeks.

"I've forgotten to say that the Gila Monster who gave me such a scare comes out every morning and suns himself. I've taken to picking him gingerly by the tail and putting him on the back of my desk where he lies out at full length in the sun. Sometimes he snaps up an unwanted fly and seems to enjoy himself greatly. I cease to fear him, though it will be long before I shall consider him handsome. I stroke his scaly back with a pencil and he likes it apparently. Some day I'll try to make him mad. I want to know if it is true about the `blowing.'"

It was almost two weeks before she pursued her experiment with the monster.

Monday, December 13, "Made my Gila monster mad enough to seize the pencil firmly between his teeth and bite it. Aside from a broken pencil, for I broke it trying to make him let go, no damage was done and I teased him with that pencil a good half day at intervals before he showed any special sign of temper. But he did not blow."

The next day she had success. "My Gila monster `blew' today, and I honestly believe if a person was in a tight room, and one of them puffed that terrible breath nearly in their face, that the person would die. It nearly killed me and I was sick most of the afternoon to pay for it. But I've learned that it is not a fable by any means." One wonders what her students were doing throughout these various antics as their teacher played with the critter. Presumably it brought much delight and laughter to break the monotony of the classroom day. Soon after her first encounter Angie became aware of other Gila monsters in the vicinity.

November 13th, "Today I saw another Gila Monster. One of Mrs. Vineyard's hens, she has only a very few, stole her nest and is setting near a rock pile. Willie found her a few days ago and today as we went past I showed it to Clara. To the surprise of us all, a Gila not quite as large as yesterday's ran out and into the rocks. On investigation we found it had eaten up all the eggs but one, but the hen who was close by had not been harmed."

The social life of families in the late 19th century consisted of much visitation back and forth among neighbors and friends. Angie Mitchell's earlier daily record while still in Prescott reflected this primary form of entertainment, but in the territorial capital there were churches to attend with "sermon tasting" almost a sport. There were balls, concerts and dramatic productions at several theaters and halls and there were dozens of saloons where people congregated to create gossip and sometimes violent acts. However, these more sophisticated outlets were not available to Tonto Basin families and the movement of people among themselves became a primary diversion. During the rest of November the teacher recorded such daily events. We share them here in order to preserve many of the names.

"Nov. 12 - Redman and young Dave Harer came this evening, the first another brother and the second a nephew, son of James I believe. There must be more Harers and their sons and grandsons than the patriarch Abraham had descendants. Dave Jr. is married and has several children but I guess they are in Phoenix.

"<u>Sunday Nov 14</u> Read awhile. Then Sarah and I went to walk & were gone a long time, till way after dark. Carter Hazelton came at noon. Redman & D. Harer Jr. left today.

"<u>Mon Nov 15</u> 24 scholars (in school). Alice's eyes too sore for her to come. John Cline came to the school house at noon & brought me some cash from Mr. Hancock and I paid Mrs. H. my board tonight." Apparently the county school board subsidized the Tonto Basin school.

"Nov 16 [Tuesday] Belle who has been staying at Mrs. H's (Hazelton's) went home unexpectedly last night. Don't know what is wrong. We've been out of candles again for several days and are burning twisted rags in bacon grease again and it is not as brilliant as gas - quite. Green & Redman H. came today.

"Nov 19 [Friday] Mrs. Hazelton is worrying greatly about Carter who started to Blake's the other day and was coming back again right off. So Sarah and I walked over to Mrs. Hook's camp to send Tom Fowler in search of him. Mrs. Hook returned this evening from Phoenix."

Note, Tom and John Fowler were sons of Mrs. Hook from a former marriage. The 1880 census, taken earlier that year, listed John Fowler, born in 1833, at the Whipple Barracks in Prescott.

"Nov. 20 [Saturday] Tom F. came at 4. Reports Carter all right and that he went to Phoenix with Dave Jr., Jasper and the rest.

"Nov 23 [Tuesday] Sarah and I went to V's (and later the other girls came) this evening.

"Nov 25 Thanksgiving Day Last eve while sitting near Mrs. Hazelton's camp fire I got a spark in my eye and oh how it hurt. It has burned it again, only it's the other eye, just as the fire did in the woods at home and such a night as I spent. Today it is a little better. This eve Sarah and I walked up to Mrs. Crabtree's to say goodbye and to return a book, as they go to Phoenix tomorrow to live. This has been a wretched Thanksgiving."

Note in the Prescott segment of Angie's diary she was caught in a forest fire outside of town and had a similar injury to one of her eyes.

"<u>Nov 26 [Friday]</u> I can't say that my walk improved my eye, as I can't do anything at all with it. Not even open it. So Sarah taught for me today, and got along nicely.

"<u>Nov 27 [Saturday]</u> After enduring an indescribable amount of misery with my eye last night – it felt about midnight as tho' a spike was sticking up in the middle of the eye – so I forced the lid up and succeeded in getting hold of something much longer and larger than any eye winker could be and that felt rough – probably a bit of half burned wood and such a relief as it was. I fell asleep and today my eye is nearly well, only weak. Cut and fitted dresses for Alice and Clara."

Chapter 17
A Hike Almost Ends in Disaster

The first teacher of Tonto Basin School, Angie Mitchell, found that her social life was rather limited among the several families that were within walking distance. Much of her leisure time was spent with her students, a number of whom actually lived with her in the teacherage or nearby at the Vineyard's ranch. Her weekends were often spent sharing her hobbies with these young people, especially her love of exploring prehistoric sites. Saturday, December 4th, dawned "wet and cold" after a hard rain during the night and so she stayed home to "wash and sort and label my specimens, of which there are quite a few."

The next day, Sunday, the weather invited a hike. Of her roommates, who were visiting elsewhere, only 14 year old Sarah Armer was left to accompany Angie. They crossed Tonto Creek and headed up into the Sierra Ancha.

Her diary records, in her own vivid way, the harrowing experience that was to follow. "We climbed one mountain after another till at 3:30 we stood on the summit of the range several miles from home. We started back down a canon that looked as if it would be a pretty easy path, and first thing we knew found ourselves in a box canon where we wouldn't be able to climb the sides in a hurry. Well, we discussed the situation & concluded we might as well see this canon through as try to retrace our steps. It was dark now with only the stars, but not at all cloudy.

"Such a trip as we had. We fell over steep rocky places twice and landed once on a big smooth sloping rock that rolled us gracefully to the bottom of the coldest spring of water I think I ever sat down in. The second time we were walking along & talking, feeling our way as cautiously as we could, when suddenly Sarah said, `Oh!' And clutching wildly at me to save herself, pulled me with her and the force with which we lit in a sandy place several feet below would be difficult to describe. I think it loosened all my teeth and I'm sure it almost `dislocated,' as Johnny would say, my spine. Sarah declares she turned a summersault and stood so long on her head that she `flattened it out' on top and quite `unsettled her brains,' but her mother says she didn't have any brain to unsettle or she wouldn't have been out there.

"Then we got among a lot of saguaros & our arms bear witness to the closeness with which they grew where we had to pass between them. Then we got a big shock. A large dusky shape near the canon wall stopped, growled & then sprang away from us with a shriek we know to be a cougar's. He was probably frightened at our rather light colored dresses, for Sarah's was a creamy looking ground with a dark spot in it, wool, and mine a very light tan. Anyway he left our neighborhood.

"We disturbed a rattlesnake in uncomfortably close proximity to our faces and left him rattling out his displeasure while we fled as fast as our uncertain ground would let us. Finally after what seemed a week we reached a place where nothing seemed to be ahead of us. Our sticks with which we poked the atmosphere touched nothing. We lay down and prodded down below with much the same result, only they hit what appeared to be a wall of rock at both sides and straight back underneath us. But nothing could we reach below. Then we tied them together with a handkerchief and tried again with like result. Sarah suggested we let ourselves down as far as possible and then jump as that seemed to be our only chance to `get out of that canon tonight.' She argued it can't be much worse than where we've already been.

"I nearly accepted her plan but somehow that deep yawning pit of blackness scared me out of the notion. Then noticing that the wall of the canon seemed, after rising some twenty feet or so, to slope back on one side (tho it might only prove to be the way starlight shone against it). I proposed we try pulling ourselves up by the brush and rocks till we passed the nearly perpendicular part and see if we couldn't get out that way. This was on the whole more feasible, so at it we went and by the skin of our teeth we passed slowly up the face of the canon wall for 20 or 25 feet. We found that it began to slope gradually up till it formed another mountain side, but not a precipitous one. We worked our way slowly and surely among the brush and cactus on this mountain, and around the side of it till we reached where we could begin to descend it.

"Soon we found ourselves in the bed of a dry, sandy creek which we soon recognized as one a couple of miles from our home. We went a little ways down it, round the bend made by the mountain, and were struck suddenly with two facts. First, the canon we had passed thro' and which had ended so abruptly was one that ended in a peculiar creamy looking ledge of rocks between two mountains, the top of this ledge being over 60 ft above the level of the sand we were on. At the very bottom of the ledge was a jagged lot of rocks. The ledge was worn as smooth as glass by the water that in the rainy seasons fell over it, like a young Niagara into the creek in whose bed we were now standing. We had seen the curious looking ledge before several times, and <u>that</u> was the place we had so nearly jumped off of! No wonder we shuddered at the thought of the fate we so narrowly escaped.

"The second thing that struck us was a big bonfire on Cactus Mountain, and it occurred to us that the folks thought us lost over on the other side in which case the fire would guide us home. It did not take us long to reach home. We found it was past 11 (we started before 8 that morning) and that they had built bon fires and shot off Vineyard's gun and shouted hoping at attract our attention. Finally Vineyard and his man had gone out in search of us and if we got back in the meantime a fire was to be built on the hill next to Cactus Mountain.

"So they built that fire and Mrs. Harer got us some supper, for we'd eaten nothing since breakfast.

Then we `took account of stock' in the way of bruises & tatters and found something less than a thousand cuts, tears and bruises; picked out several hundred cactus & catclaw thorns from different parts of our anatomy, put on several feet of court plaster and gave up our wardrobe as past mending and got into other clothes.

"We came as near being total wrecks as we well could be. John V. soon came and when we told him where we'd been he said, `That canon: why I wouldn't come down it for any money. It's a miracle you're alive.' We shortly after crawled into bed and hope to be O.K. in the morning."

The next day Angie described her aches and pains. "O yes! We're O. K.! Or perhaps the reverse - `K. O.' would more nearly express our state of body and mind. We are so stiff we can scarcely crawl, and if we bend over it is nearly impossible to straighten up. If we once get up it seems equally difficult to bend over again. School ran smoothly, but it was hard to teach today for I felt so like a busted community."

By Wednesday she could report, "Am all right once more except for a few remaining scratches. Sarah ditto."

Chapter 18
Early Visitors to Tonto Cliff Dwellings

Just one week after teacher Angie Mitchell's fateful hike into the mountains that nearly took her life she eagerly tackled another weekend adventure.

After school on Friday, December 10, Sarah Armer and her teacher went with Mrs. Hazelton and two children to the Hook ranch to obtain a horse they planned to use on a Saturday excursion. On the way home they "explored some ruins and did not get home till long after the others."

Saturday turned out differently. Anticipating the months ahead when she would be back in Prescott, Angie applied for a clerkship with the Territorial Legislature. Saturday she received a message in that regard, though she did not record the contents in her diary. Instead, she stayed home and taught school "to make up a lost day." At sunset "Alice, Clara, Melinda and I started to Armer's on Salt River and got there quite late." [1] The plan was to spend the night there and get an early start in the morning for some cliff dwellings Angie had heard about along the Salt River.

"Dec 12th [Sunday] We ate breakfast long before day and were well on our way at sunrise. I rode `Salim,' a horse of Mr. Armer's. Melinda rode Brownie, the one I got from Hook, as he is not quite as gentle as Salim and Melinda is a first-class rider while I'm not of late years. We went 5 ½ miles or so to the foot of Ute Mountain in which the 'caves' are located. [2] We fastened our horses to brush and climbed the mountain, which was by no means an easy task as it is covered with debris from the ruined walls. One slides back a good deal like the `frog in the well' who jumped `two feet forward & then fell back three.' [3] But we finally reached the dwellings. It was far superior to what I had anticipated & worth the trouble.

"The dwelling is built of small rocks laid in cement and is cemented inside and out and sets well back beneath an overhanging rock. The rock is, I should think, about 200 feet high and curves over something like this. [She sketched a side view of a pueblo under an overhanging rock.] We found traces of 33 rooms and some 18 of them are in fair preservation. It has been seven or eight stories high, or perhaps more, I should think judging from the poles still clinging high up to the rock. There was originally no opening in the outer wall but the dwellers in the house climbed up a ladder of some sort and went in at the second story, as the Zunis and kindred tribes do yet! One room is walled up solidly without any door opening into it. Of course one can enter it now from above for the ceiling is partly fallen in. Another had a door originally but for some reason the people living there decided to close that room also and so smoothly and well was the work done that not a trace of any doorway having ever been there can be seen from outside the room. But inside of it one can easily see the rocks filling in the doorway, laid up in cement but not cemented over on the inside. When the ceiling of this room was intact, after the door was walled up, it must have been nearly air tight and one wonders why it was done. It is located in a rather central situation in the second story. One can conjecture several reasons. It may have been to hide treasure, to hide a crime, to punish a criminal or for several other reasons.

"In one room in the first story a Mr. Danforth (I think is the name) two years ago this winter found the skeleton of an infant in the wall about 5 ft from the floor, or possibly a little less. [4] I saw the place today. The child was wrapped in many folds of a silky looking cotton cloth, like some we found in the same room. Tom says (and he was here when the child was found) the material had a kind of drawn pattern in small diamonds and stars, and had shredded bark in its mouth and ears like a mummy, and sandals of yucca fiber on its feet made like a pair we dug from another part of the ruin only very much smaller. Then there were some turquoise and red pipe-clay beads, clay toys, a doll and dog, and bone ornaments with it. Also a number of other trifles. The place in which it lay was hollowed out of the wall and cemented inside smoothly. Then the tiny corpse was laid in and a few rocks laid up in cement hid it forever from its parents, and then the outside was smoothly cemented till it could not be distinguished from the rest of the wall."

In the course of this chapter Angie refers to Tom, Frank and Bud. These lads were Armers. In the 1880 census Tom was 10, Frank was 8, and "Bud" (probably James) was 6. Tom Armer would become head of the family after their father died in 1909 and during World

War I he was elected sheriff of Gila County. He ran cattle on their range above Roosevelt Lake.

Frank Armer never married and in his early 20s participated in a train robbery that landed him in the Territorial Prison at Yuma. During an escape attempt he was shot and the resulting lung ailment caused his death in 1909. James Armer would marry Mary Margaret Chilson from Payson.

Angie's diary continues. "Another room has on its eastern wall a hieroglyphic representing probably the sun and some other lines that might be anything. In several places are prints of fingers or of the hand complete and perfect as the day ages ago when the hands were pressed into the plastic clay. There is much to be seen in the building that I've not time to speak of. One ought to stay a week to explore it if they hope to satisfy their curiosity."

She continues to describe a second cliff house, separated from the first by "a gulch... It is the most perfect I've ever seen, with traces of 22 rooms. 16 are in fair order, 3 of them and a hall are as perfect as the day they were finished. The hall is a narrow space between two rooms and has a short flight of steps leading to a tiny landing on the upper floor. The stairs are quite wide but very low, not more than 3 ¼ to 4 ¼ inches I should think in height, from one step to the next, and so worn by the myriad feet that ascended and descended them as to be hollow troughs in the center.

"We were rambling around one of the upper story rooms exclaiming on the extremely fine state of preservation it was in, when Clara saw something in a dark corner she wanted to look at and started toward it. The floor was covered with various sorts of trash several inches deep and she `waded' towards the corner. Suddenly there was a scream and the place where Clara had stood was vacant, but certainly not silent for heartrending cries came from below. For a minute we stood nearly petrified with fright and then I flew out of the room and down the stairs to a room opening from the landing on the east side. Poking my candle in, I beheld Clara, hysterical from her scare, sitting in an immense heap of chollas that filled the room half way to the ceiling & were evidently stored there by rats, tho for what purpose I'm sure I can't guess. Truly this was appalling! But when Clara saw that she could reach the door by crawling thro' that agonizing pile of thorns she bravely stopped crying and started. The only aid any one could give her was to hold the candle so she could see and that I did. If we had had a rope we might have lowered it down the aperture she fell through and pulled her up. It would have been less painful. But there was no rope, so she crawled out and if we had not been frightened at the consequences of so many cholla thorns in the poor child's tender flesh we would certainly have laughed for a more ridiculous object was never seen.

"The chollas were all over her clothes, her limbs and her hair and piled up 8 and 10 deep till she was a walking stack of them. Well, we took her and pulled off all the big ones till we reached the inner layer, which was attached principally to her skin. And then trouble for us and agony for her began in earnest. Of course the cruel, hooked barbs broke from the cholla rather than let go the flesh and after we finally got the last whole cholla off she still had scores of those thorns all over her, excepting her face. Then we girls half led, half carried her to an empty room, one where there was not much debris, though dust of course. Spread my big waterproof down on the floor, stripped her and two of us, Alice & I, picked and cut and pulled out all the cholla we could while Melinda got all the thorns possible out of her clothes. We had part of a bottle of milk left from lunch and we rubbed her with that. It eased the pain a little. She dressed and we took her to a cozy corner outside under some mesquite, rolled her up snugly in our cloaks and she sobbed herself to sleep. Melinda, who had made several trips to the cave, so to whom it was an old story, offered to stay with her while Alice and I continued exploring. So we returned to the ruins and after spending another half hour getting the cholla out of our hands, which we had got in pulling them at first off Clara, we began (exploring) where we left off. Tom & Frank & Bud had examined the upper room and the place Clara fell thro' was an opening for a trap door. Probably there used to be a ladder extending to the lower floor. Our cholla incident had taken a long two hours, so we hurried up our inspection. We found many finger prints here too, and a room that evidently had been a kitchen. The floor is formed partly by a big rock (which also forms part of the side) and in this rock were ½ a dozen metates hollowed out of it and varying in size, depth & shape. This rock wall and the ceiling above were black with smoke and there was a quantity of ashes etc. in it."

As the sun was setting the little company built a camp fire and prepared supper, capped by "bread and butter, pie and cookies" that Mrs. Armer had sent along. In a fitting summary of the experience, Angie's imagination identifies with the prehistoric people. "It seemed strange to be chatting and laughing so gaily in a house built unknown centuries ago by people unlike us in appearance but who had known joy and grief, pleasure and pain same as our race of today knows them, and who had laughed, cried, sung, danced, married & died, mourned or rejoiced their lives away in this once populous town, or castle, or whatever one would call it! It made an uncanny feeling come over us as we rested till moon rise and talked of this long dead people and told the little we knew concerning them. "By & by the moon rose & softened the marks of time on the scarred, weather stained cliff dwellings till it was beautiful."

They reached the Armer ranch about 9:30, "tired but happy. Even Clara, sore as she was, declaring she was glad that she went. Mrs. Armer had supper waiting & we did justice to our second one after our ride." Heading on home from there, Angie and her "children" (as she calls them) got home after midnight and were soon asleep.

The young teacher adds the next day, "Armer fairly made me promise to teach the spring term. I'm glad he is suited." However, she was anticipating returning to her fiancé in Prescott and probably had no intention of returning for another session of Tonto School.

NOTES:

[1] Sara and Melinda Armer are listed in the 1880 census as 14 and 13, just as Angie reports them. Melinda would die while still a teenager.

[2] Her reference to "Ute Mountain" is obscure, since there is no such place name in Gila County. The Ute Mountains in Arizona are far to the west in Mojave County. However, she proceeds to describe in detail the cliff dwellings that today are named The Tonto National Monument, near Roosevelt Lake. When this author submitted Angie's description to the Ranger archaeologists at the Tonto National Monument, they confirmed the location, and were grateful to have this firsthand account of how the cliff dwellings appeared in 1880.

[3] It is possible Angie has confused several fables here. "The Frog in the Well" is both an Irish jig and a Chinese fable, having to do with a frog who sees only the sky above from his well and has no notion of the vast ocean beyond. There is nothing in it about "two feet forward and falling back three." It is also possible that the idea of a frog falling into a well and fruitlessly trying to escape was a contemporary saying.

[4] The Danforth family lived in Richmond Basin, a ghost town today between Tonto Basin and Globe. In 1880 it was a ranching area and later became a silver mining camp. George Danforth was born about 1830 in Massachusetts.

Chapter 19
Preparations to Leave Tonto

Wednesday, December 15, 1880 was the last day of the fall session at the Tonto Basin School. The families of the students arrived to help close the school and take their children home that evening. Teacher Angie reported a gloomy, rainy day.

"School closed today. It rained awfully, but the whole Armer family, George Moore, [1] and Hook, Mr. and Mrs. Harer, Mrs. Hazelton, the Vineyards, Fannie, Laura and Adeline Gordon came at 9:30 and stayed till the close. I've an idea now about how much room Noah had left in the Ark. 19 pupils and myself, and 18 more counting two babies, this is a good many on a rainy day in a room 10 by 12 feet. I don't quite know how we did it. After school Sarah and I cleaned everything up inside as well as we could, barricaded the doorway with boards, and went home and packed up for the Phoenix trip."

The plan was for the Harers to accompany her to Phoenix where she would catch the stage for Prescott. Her aim was to be home for Christmas. To celebrate the close of the school session, "all of us girls went to Vineyard's and staid till 10:30."

She added a comment that indicated she wanted to keep her options open for the future. "The trustees reengaged me to teach next term. School to begin 1st Monday in February, if I don't get my clerkship [in the Territorial Legislature]."

117

Getting started on the trip to Phoenix was difficult as the rain continued all night Thursday and was still raining on Friday. Apparently the brushy roof of the house where Angie was living became saturated because Thursday afternoon "a rafter broke and I tell you the men put props under our roof in a hurry."

David Harer announced in the morning that he had waited as long as he could and even though the rain continued they would proceed. "It certainly met my approval for I want to get home for Christmas and can't if we wait any longer."

By 1 o'clock it had stopped raining and the sun shone so they launched their trip. "We thought it might be that the storm was over but we were mistaken for we had just reached Hooks, two and a half miles from home, when it rained as though the bottom of the bucket had fallen out. Right there we had to stop at 4:30. It had taken 3 and a half hours to go two and a half miles, and I guess at that rate we'll reach Phoenix in time for me to get home next 4th of July. I never saw such mud anywhere; it equals the Puerco." The Puerco River is in New Mexico and Angie remembered passing through that area when her family came from the east.

The Phoenix bound party had two wagons and included John Vineyard driving his wagon with Mrs. Hazelton. Harer's wagon included the elder Harers, Sarah, Reggie, Abbie and Angie. She adds, "My little dog Onyx is also a passenger on our train." This Newfoundland puppy had been given to Angie right after Thanksgiving by the Gordon family who owned the mother and were giving the puppies to other ranch families. On November 29th her diary had recorded, "He is a perfectly little beauty and I named him Onyx." The name may have referred to the color of his coat.

The continuing rain hampered their travels. They spent the night at the Hook ranch and it rained all night again. The next day, Saturday, December 18 they started out again with intermittent rain and "got to Reno after dark, 17 and a half miles from Hooks. We started at 6:30 and Sarah and I walked 12 miles. Waded would more correctly express it, I guess." That night they slept on the kitchen floor at the Reno station, where "Mr. and Mrs. Smith who keep the station were very kind to us."

A post office had been established at the site of Old Camp Reno the previous October with Mr. Isaac R. Prather the postmaster. Prather and his brother had established a store at Reno and the post office was the first one in Tonto Basin. The Smiths were hosts to those who stayed the night. Sunday morning the travelers headed out again and reached the top of the mountain by nightfall. The diary describes their day's travel.

"Cold as Greenland up here, and so windy. We traveled fairly well today. Went over Reno Hill, past Sunflower Valley, and to the top of Sunflower Mountain. Got there after dark and they were afraid to try to go down the hill as it is not the best road on earth. So we camped on top of Sunflower, of all places on earth! It is like the roof, a long sloping roof, of a house and about as level on top as a ridge pole. Almost any way you go is down hill. Oh! It's a daisy!"

She later reported that though they had "piles of blankets we all froze out." She indicated the uneven ground was like a cone and so narrow they had to divide up sleeping on the several slopes. "After an hour or two's vain chase of our blankets and bed to keep them from rolling down the hill, we had an inspiration and drove some sticks into the ground, tying the bedding to them.... When we wakened half frozen it was to find ourselves several feet down hill with a solitary blanket which had managed to get free and it mostly on the ground. We were entirely on the ground with our heads against a bush. Mrs. Hazelton had gravitated downward with Regie and was occupying the place supposed to be ours. We gave it up then and Mr. Harer, who came nearer swearing than I ever heard him, crawled out about the same time and declared he was freezing. So we set to work to get a fire, if we could, and at last succeeded. We built a tremendous one and the rest got up and we all sat there till daylight."

Monday was fortunately somewhat warmer and they reached the Verde River at Fort McDowell just at dark. The teacher's description of crossing the Verde is classic Angie Mitchell writing. "The stream was running pretty swiftly and to me it looked very deep. But our wagon set up high and Harer certainly is not afraid of water, though he's usually careful too. Mrs. H. objected to crossing till morning, but he didn't want to wait. So finally he dove in. We have four good stout horses and one of the leaders is a very large, powerful stallion named Prince. When we got to the middle of the river the current swept us down away from the ford and toward the Mormon Dam. [2] The leaders lost their heads, the water poured into the wagon and on we swept. Nearer the dam which boomed like a small Niagara, Abbie cried but I cuddled him close to me and covered his eyes, and he ceased crying. Mr. Harer shouted all sorts of things to his horses, and Mrs. H and I never spoke. It was awful. Suddenly Prince pulled himself up and commenced to exert all his great strength to reach shallower water. There came shouts from the bank near the fort, and a soldier urged his horse out a little way from the bank, and threw a lariat, caught one of the horses and commenced pulling in the same direction Prince was. That saved us. Soon we were in shallow water and a little later safely ashore. John V. saw part of our struggle, then the landing, indistinctly as it was getting pretty dark. He concluded to camp where he was like a sensible fellow."

NOTES:

[1] **George Moore was 24 years old and single, a miner who worked locally, perhaps for the Armers. He had come from Iowa.**

[2] **This is not to be confused with the later Mormon Flat Dam, built on the Salt River creating Canyon Lake. Angie's reference is to a small diversion dam near Ft. McDowell on the lower Verde River. The name comes from the fact that about this same time Mormon settlers grazed their livestock in the area.**

Chapter 20
A Visit with Captain and Mrs. Chaffee

The trip home to Prescott from Tonto Basin was almost as difficult as her trip over the Rim to Tonto Basin four months earlier. Having reached the Verde River opposite Fort McDowell, the party of two wagons barely made it across the raging waters, the teacher and her driver, Mr. Harer, being almost dragged under when the wagon was pulled downstream by the current. The other wagon, driven by John Vineyard, waited patiently and crossed the next morning when daylight made navigation easier.

"Dec 21 [Tuesday] My trunk came over in John's wagon so of course it was all right. This morning I went up to see Annie Chaffee for an hour or two. The Major is in command at the Post here."

Cavalry officer Adna R. Chaffee would lead one of several regiments in the Battle of Big Dry Wash, July 17, 1882. It was the last pitched battle between U. S. troops and the Apache Indians in Arizona Territory. A renegade group, primarily Tonto Apaches, had broken from the San Carlos and White Mountain Reservations and left a trail of blood and burned ranches until they were met by Army forces on top of the Mogollon Rim. [1]

It rained Monday night again and continued Tuesday morning which delayed her visit to the Chaffees. However, Angie's concern to be properly dressed for such a visit also held them up. Her diary continues, "I had not intended going to Chaffee's for of course I can't `dress up.' And tho' my dress is a pretty, gray wool yet it is rumpled. (I got it out of my trunk this morn, to replace the one the water ruined yesterday and threw the other one into the river!) And of course I'm not so very spick and span that I'm anxious to go calling on the Post Commandant's wife, but someone told Chaffee about a team crossing the Verde last night and how near the occupants came to drowning. When he asked who they were he said, `I don't know, they're people from Tonto Basin and one is the school ma'am from there.' Whereupon the Major said, `My goodness!' And considerably to the other's surprise came straight to our camp. I had gone over behind a pile of boards and was sitting watching the river, which is rising all the time, when I heard the Major say, `Are there some teams from Tonto here?' (There are about 20 teams camped in and near the corral.) I recognized his voice but decided to keep still. Harer said, "Yes sir, two of us."

`Have you Miss Mitchell with you?'

`Yes sir!'

`Well, I'd like to see her. Where shall I find her?'

That they couldn't answer, so the Major strode round the boards on the way to the river thinking, as he said, `I might have gone there, and almost walked over her.' He stopped, held out his hand & said, `What kind of a trick is this you're playing us? Annie has had me overhaul every granger from the Reno country for two weeks hunting you and now you are going straight through without stopping.' [2] He was shaking hands and smiling while scolding. `Now you are coming with me this minute, so give somebody an order to get your luggage and I'll have a fellow here after it in ten minutes."

"But Major, I can't stop at all. I have to get to Phoenix as soon as possible; besides look at my costume. I can't go to Annie's this way."

"He argued well but finally gave up and we compromised by my going to see Annie and staying a couple of hours. I found she expected me to spend Christmas with her and I would have been glad to but knew I was obliged to head home. It seems she had sent me a letter on the subject, which I never received and soon explained matters. I spent two delightful hours and Annie was very kind to Sarah too. Then we started once more and reached Carley's (or some similar name) ranch about dark and camped. But it began to rain very hard and Mr. C., who is a bachelor and an old friend of the Harers, insisted on our coming in and staying inside instead of camping. I claimed it was due to Sarah's attractive manner, and we had a good deal of fun. It was very pleasant tho' and tonight we made our beds down on the floor of the big room (some 30 ft x 18) of the house."

The next day, Wednesday December 22, Angie continued describing their trip to Phoenix where she hoped to catch the stage. "It rained most of the night, but this morning is pleasant tho' the mud is absolutely without bottom. Started fairly early but only got to the neighborhood of Tempe and camped tonight near a Mexican's house, as it is the only place one can get good drinking water, every ditch is so muddy. The Mexican came out to camp and talked to Mr. Harer, and after he went back she (the Senora) sent a message inviting the `Senoras' to come up to the porch which was dry. We went; it was clean and we were muddy, but she insisted, so shedding our rubbers we went up and soon she brought us a brush to brush the mud from our shoes if we wished as we most certainly did wish to. My skirt is quite short and I had had the luck not to get it muddy. Sarah's had little on it but Mrs. Hazelton's was pretty wet and drabbled [3], and Mrs. Harer was also. The senora did not appear to care and invited us into the house... She speaks a little English, I a little Spanish (Sarah doesn't know any yet) and we pretended to understand. She watched me so closely it was uncomfortable, and paid some attention to Sarah... When we came out to go to camp where the men had supper ready she stepped up & kissed me Spanish style to my great surprise. Sarah and I discussed it and concluded I must resemble some dear friend. I'm tanned enough to resemble any Mexican!"

Apparently the Spanish speaking hostess took a fancy to Angie and sent word by "a fine looking lad" that she was invited to dinner. Mrs. Hazelton, Angie reported, got "in a bad humor" over Angie being preferred. When she did not go to the ranch house a second young lad was sent to insist she come. The invitation was addressed to "the young lady" and they thought it might be Sarah but the messenger bowed to Angie and spoke in Spanish. Mrs. Harer helped translate. "'She wanted the one with the red lips, the eyes & the hands.' I giggled and so did Sarah, as if we didn't both possess those! Mrs. H. continued, `He says the tall young lady, and she wants her to come up for awhile as she will have some friends arrive soon and she thinks the young lady may enjoy it.'"

"`Didn't she ask us both?' I inquired. `No, only you. She has, he tells me, taken a great fancy to you & will be really grieved if you refuse.' I thought a minute and Sarah urged me to go. I decided I'd see what a Mexican evening party might be like."

With that Angie went to the wagon and changed her clothes, while Sarah fixed her hair.

"The young fellow had put some boards down from the camp to the walk inside the gate (about 50 ft I guess) and I got there without getting at all muddy. He led me to his mother who kissed me twice, then introduced the boys as Ramon and Manuel. She insisted on my eating some `dulcies' [4] and drinking some coffee in spite of my assurance that I was not hungry. Then Ramon took a guitar and played and she showed me a number of curiosities from old Mexico and from Arizona ruins. She seemed delighted to find that specimens were something I delighted in. After that a dozen young senors and senoritas arrived and I found they were celebrating some kind of a fete day; the Senora's birth, wedding, or something. They seemed surprised to see me and well they might be. But she introduced me to them as kindly as if I were a long lost relative just arrived. I grew bewildered between Senorita Carmen, Senorita Manuela, Senorita Panchita till I thought my head would surely grow dizzy. There was Senor Juan and Senor Francisco and Senor Pedro and Senor Rafael and half a dozen more with unpronounceable names attached. We had music, singing also, dancing and games till we were all tired. Then refreshments of all sorts of dulcies, preserves, bread, chicken tamales, and some sort of Mexican liquor, coffee and chocolate. At last I said I must go and they came over and bade me goodnight, or `Buenos noches,' one by one and wished me a pleasant journey and a speedy return to Tonto (as I had promised to stay a day on my way to the Basin if I could). And the girls kissed me Spanish style, and the young men shook hands. Then the Senora went on the porch with me and kissed me again and Ramon took me home. I certainly had had a jolly time. I crawled in, after getting into my flannel gown, beside Sarah & was soon sound asleep."

NOTES:

[1] At the time of the battle in 1882 Chaffee was listed as a captain so it is likely that Angie, two years earlier, had mistakenly given him the rank of major. The location of the battle was called "Big Dry Wash" in Major Evans' official report, but later maps called the location "Big Dry Fork".

[2] A "granger" was a farmer. Mrs. Chaffee welcomed passing civilians and enjoyed their company and news

from "the outside." It is clear here that the Chaffees had met Angie or heard of her before and knew she was coming this way.

[3]To become wet and dirty.

[4]Dulce is the Spanish word for "sweet."

Chapter 21
A Race to Get Home for Christmas

Teacher Angie Mitchell was heading home to Prescott and had gotten as far as Tempe on an adventurous trip from Tonto Basin. Several folks from Tonto accompanied her with their wagons as she headed for Phoenix where the stage could be boarded for Prescott. Intense rain plagued them all the way and caused their progress to be slow again. They camped outside of Phoenix at the ranch of a very gracious Mexican family. Her diary continues.

"<u>Dec 23rd [Thursday]</u> This morning we were up early and just after our breakfast the Senora appeared. After talking to all of us said she had some "panoche" at the house for me to take home if I wished. [1] I <u>did</u> wish, took Sarah with me and went up with Senora to the house. She talked to us and once in a while we understood. She took us out to her cellar, and it was a nice one too, full of preserves, jams, jars of butter and of panoche and all sorts of things mostly in pottery ollas and large bowls. She gave me a gallon crock of panoche, and said I'd find the crock or olla handy about the house. She also gave us some preserves made of the `wild date' for dinner and then gave me some specimens for my cabinet. I was aghast at the size of the crock of panoche and wanted to pay but she said, `No, no,' and seemed so hurt that I thanked her the best I could. She went back to our camp and carried the panoche for me. We found a box & got some hay &

packed it well. Then she told me [and Mrs.] Harer that if I wanted a good tamale recipe she'd give me one. I wanted it, for hers last night were the finest I had ever eaten, so she told it to Mrs. H and she translated and I wrote it. Then she brought out a cheese of goat's milk and added that to our bill of fare for dinner. Soon after (that) we left and reached Phoenix about 11. Hancock had letters for me from home and Geo. and I sent the folks a telegram. [2] We are stopping at Dave Harer's. We stopped at Capt Sharp's to see him about my clerkship and he promised to help all he could." [3]

They spent the night at Dave Harer's and the next day was Christmas Eve. Angie did some shopping in the town, perhaps buying gifts for her family in anticipation of getting home the next day. She was disappointed to find the stage for Prescott was full and she would have to wait until the next day, Christmas Day. A friend of David Harer's, George H. Rothrock, invited her to attend a dance with him that evening. "I accepted gladly, for I can't go home till tomorrow at 2 a.m. as the stage is full. Couldn't have gone tomorrow if some, kindly faced old miner hadn't given me his place; said he guessed he'd just as soon spend Christmas one place as another and he knew the `little gal' wanted to get home. When I thanked him, he said, `Never mind that part of it. I like to see a gal anxious to git home and am glad to help her if I can."

That night she danced until after midnight and found "several girls and one or two men" she knew, making it a very enjoyable evening. After the dance she "went to Harer's, changed my clothes, stuffed my traps in the trunk, got it and my satchel ready to go to the (stage) office. In a minute an express came for them and then I rolled little Onyx up in his blanket, took my warm pair of blankets and plenty of wraps and bid the family goodbye. A few minutes later the stage came and I found I was the 5th inside passenger, one old lady and three men being the others."

The first leg of her journey got her to the stage coach office in the heart of town. The stage was a little late and they did not arrive at the main stage office until after three o'clock in the morning. There they found another problem blocking a smooth trip home. "The Manager was in a puzzle. He had promised to send some luggage belonging to the theatrical troupe that went up yesterday on this stage... but the passengers insisted their luggage had to go sure. Every man had a trunk and Mrs. Rupert, the other lady, had a Saratoga and I had a trunk. I also had 2 boxes, small and medium to go when they could, and the stage would only hold so much. [4] He appealed to the men but they refused to give way. The Troupe's baggage was prepaid and they needed it badly for the performance billed for Monday, and he couldn't get it to them otherwise. Mrs. Rupert declared she could not wait. I said nothing while I revolved (sic) the situation and then said, `Well, I've not expected to have to leave my trunk and it's extremely inconvenient, but as the next stage will be in Tuesday, you may leave my baggage all behind except the satchel.'"

Angie pointed out that even with her two trunks waiting over there still would not be room for all the people who wanted on that stage. However, in the light of her generosity nobility rose to the surface, "The youngest man whistled a minute or two and burst out, `Oh hang it all, if the young lady can wait four days I reckon I can. You may leave mine.' Then the older of the other two said, `It's deuced inconvenient. I can wait, and you may leave my luggage too.' So the Troupe's trunks were piled on with Mrs. Rupert's and the 3rd man's. Just as I was leaving the room the Agent said, `Miss Mitchell, I'll send both boxes and your trunk on Tuesday.' We were allowed 100# baggage and excess is 10 cents per lb. My trunk weighs 185 and the box 98 and the little box 25 so I've 208# excess and that will cost $20.80. But it can't be helped. The night was keenly cold and when we got well out onto the desert the wind grew stronger." [5]

The route from Phoenix to Prescott went by way of Wickenburg, "We rode across the desert, stopping for breakfast at Calderwood's Station and on to Wickenburg where we took supper."

Calderwood's Station was a stage stop on the road to Wickenburg near today's highway 60 and the Agua Fria River. It is in the vicinity of Surprise, Arizona and was named for Captain M. H. Calderwood, a captain in the California Volunteers. In California he had been a grocer and an assemblyman in Placer County. He came to this area during the Civil War and presumably established a grocery business.

During this stage stop to change horses, Angie's dog Onyx was stolen by "a livery stable hostler… but I got him O.K. and we finally started again." Sometime after dark they reached another station at Stanton situated at the base of Rich Hill. Charles P. Stanton founded the place and it was an important stop between Wickenburg and the difficult climb up the mountains to Prescott. Today it is a ghost town owned by the Lost Dutchman Mining Association. They use it as a base for their members to prospect for gold.

What happened during the next few hours would become one last harrowing adventure for Angie before she reached the security of home in Prescott.

NOTES:

[1] Panoche is course Mexican sugar.
[2] Hancock was the superintendent of county schools.
[3] Dave Harer, a younger son of the elder, lived at times in Tonto and in Phoenix. Angie inquires about her application to be appointed clerk of the Territorial Legislature meeting in Prescott. Her plan was to take that position rather than return to Tonto if it was offered.
[4] Mrs. E. M. Rupert had two sons at Prescott who were miners. The 1880 census states they were from "Lynch Creek", but this is probably a census taker's error meaning Lynx Creek.
[5] Prescott *Weekly Miner,* December 31, 1880, "The Nellie Boyd Troupe will give a series of popular plays for one week, commencing Saturday, December 25th, 1880. For particulars see small bills and posters." Later in that

same issue, "Nellie Boyd Troupe tonight." Apparently their trunks arrived in time, thanks to Angie.

Chapter 22
A Frightful Final Ride

Teacher Angie Mitchell completed her term at the Tonto Basin School and she was eagerly on her way home to Prescott. Her attempt to spend Christmas 1880 with her family and fiancé, George Brown, encountered one hazard after another on the trip. Now it was Christmas Day, and as the stage coach from Wickenburg headed for the last mountainous road, doom almost caught up with her.

At one stage stop outside of Phoenix her dog, Onyx, was stolen by a stable hand but she was able to retrieve him. Angie wrote, "We finally started again. All went well till we got to Stanton some time after dark and changed horses again. The teams were hay broken broncos and the new driver more than half drunk. We inside were rolled up in big cloaks and had blankets tucked around us till we were packed in like sardines. I gathered from the conversation between the two elder men that they were coming to look at some mines… and were experts. One had evidently been in the West before while it was quite new to the other… The 3rd man, the young fellow, said nothing and appeared to know neither of the others. Mrs. R [a fellow passenger], whom I knew some years ago, and I talked some but she was nervous and fidgety over the roads and I was tired from my trip and the dance. So we were rather still and I went to sleep. While the stage was going up Antelope Mountain, and pretty near the summit, there was a lurch and then a quickened motion. It woke me and it soon dawned on me that something was seriously wrong. Our team was running away!"

Angie continues to relate the harrowing ride.

"A moment later the summit was passed and our broncos, without brake or any apparent restraint, were plunging down one of the most dangerous mountain grades in the Territory with a precipice close to the road over which the coach seemed to swing clear from the road. Peering out I saw the lines dragging and then I knew - the drunken driver had fallen or been thrown off at the time the train started. The situation had dawned on my fellow passengers about the same time and such a scene as ensued! The fellow, the expert who had `been West' had evidently accumulated a varied vocabulary of oaths for he strung them out at a rate of speed I never heard equaled. He entirely forgot his precise drawl, while his friend, the Eastern expert prayed with the same wonderful flow of language. Those two kept up their swearing and praying till the end of the race. It was the most amusing concert I ever heard. Mrs. R. went off into hysterics and wept and screamed and shrieked all the way. The young fellow and myself said not a word, until becoming so amused at this chorus of howls, oaths & prayers that I could not help it. I laughed. Then he said, with a laugh also, `Poor things, they're just crazy but aren't you scared?' and I said, `Oh yes, awfully, but I can't help laughing for I never heard anything so funny and crying and howling only makes the matter worse.' Then I gazed out of the window on my side and thought sure every second we'd go over that precipice and be dashed to pieces.

"After the horses had by some Providential means escaped dashing us all on the rocks and had nearly reached the foot of the hill, the young fellow got up, opened the door and holding tightly to the swaying stage, stood a moment on the step."

Our reporter states that the three in hysterics did not even notice the fellow's noble attempt to stop the stage. "In a moment the young man swung himself up by some means to the top. There I could only see what followed by glimpses, but he crawled to the driver's seat, then down and then to the tongue and finally got the reins one at a time. The horses were still galloping swiftly but the ground was more broken and we were quite down the hill itself. (The horses) were getting winded with their long race, and presently he brought them to a full stop. It took the trio inside fully a minute to realize that the peril was past and no one was hurt. Then they subsided into silence but kept looking at each other as if each one wondered just what he had done or said and I doubt if they will ever quite realize it!

"About this time the driver, hatless and coatless (he'd thrown off both coats to run faster) appeared sobered, white faced and nearly breathless and gasped, `My God! Are they all dead inside?' We assured him we were very much alive and perfectly safe. The young man gave him his own overcoat and wrapped himself up in his blanket. Soon we started and reached Genung's, changed horses, and then on again."

At last the stage pulled into Prescott at 7:30 AM Christmas morning. Angie writes that she was "profoundly thankful to get here sound in mind and limb, tho' sore and stiff from our shaking up. George met me there and we walked out home." [1]

Angie's mother decided the family would celebrate Christmas on the Sunday December 26th since she was unsure when their daughter would get home. The diary reports "a fine dinner." Then, "I went down to Josie's about 2 and staid an hour. Tonight George and I and Josie and Joe went to church together to hear Bovard. Mrs. Kelly is ill. I had quite a number of nice presents. Onyx stood the trip nicely, but I fancy he has a cold or something. On Monday, December 27th Angie's trunk and the boxes she left back in Phoenix arrived by stage. "I went to settle for the excess baggage and found every one of them marked paid. I could not understand it, till the agent gave me a letter. On opening it I found a note from the agent at Phoenix enclosing receipt for $20.80 for amount due on baggage and the words, `Please accept as a token of my gratitude for the favor you did me on Christmas Eve by enabling me to keep my word to the Troupe. It was worth much more to me than this is to you, and if I can do you a favor at any future time don't hesitate to say so and I'll do it with pleasure.' I wrote a note of thanks and went home."

NOTES:

[1] The Mitchell family lived west of Granite Creek and south of Gurley, probably less than a mile from the center of town.

Chapter 23 Epilogue, The Wedding

Angie Mitchell returned home to Prescott on Christmas Day, 1880 after teaching at the first school in Tonto Basin. Ten days later she received word of her appointment as clerk for the House of Representatives in the 11th Arizona Territorial Legislature. She applied for this position before going to teach on Tonto Creek and promised to return for the next term unless her application in Prescott was confirmed. Now she would not return to Tonto but would remain in her hometown, "enrolling and engrossing" bills submitted in the House of Representatives.

"Enrolling" was the tedious task of writing the copy of a bill for the legislature and "engrossing" was to incorporate the amendments into the bill and then enrolling the final copy. All of this was done by hand and Angie's diary reflects late or even all night sessions in which a bill had to be ready for a vote.

One might suspect Mr. George Brown's political influence in obtaining this position for his fiancée, since he was a representative in the House for Yavapai County. However, Angie was highly respected on her own, having held teaching positions at several schools in the Prescott area. Her life both before and after the Tonto Basin term was quite sophisticated. She hobnobbed with political and community leaders, sermon tasted in Prescott's earliest established churches, attended plays and concerts, danced at the many balls in town and at Ft. Whipple, and spent countless days and evenings visiting with her peers. She was also the organist for the West Side Church (Methodist Episcopal South), located just west of Whiskey Row and Granite Creek.

In a history of the local Eastern Star chapter, its author remembers the following. "There was no night in Prescott that business did not close up for either darkness or for Sunday, but there was a reunion Sunday morning church and when Angie Mitchell began to sing and play there all the gambling houses closed tight shut for that hour and in their best clothes the proprietors went to church, listened to the really fine music, put a generous handful of coins in the contribution box, and went back to open up the most prosperous and lucky games of the week." [1]

Saturday January 1, 1881 her diary continued, "Had a number of calls from friends and also from the legislators who have already arrived…" This kind of "open house" became the rule throughout the legislative session. On Tuesday January 4th her election as Clerk of the House was formalized. Her daily diary was maintained but the brief entries are taken up primarily with her sewing projects, her visits, the weather, and George's "bad cold and sick headache."

George Brown owned a ranch on the headwaters of the Agua Fria River near the present town of Meyer. It was a long ride into town so during the sessions of the legislature he stayed with the Mitchells.

Soon after her return from Tonto Basin Angie reported that her dog Onyx developed distemper. On Sunday, January 2nd in her usual dispassionate reporting, she simply wrote, "Onyx died tonight." Although Angie could record intricate details and be enthusiastic over the adventures she had almost daily in Tonto Basin, her diary reveals no emotion regarding personal feelings. There is no expression of sorrow over the dog's death and she reported tragedies such as murders or mine accidents as mere facts. Furthermore, the details of her courtship with George Brown remained a secret.

On January 20th she reported an evening visit from someone named Hussey who offered George a bribe of $1,000 "to vote for the repeal of the Bullion Tax, but he wouldn't touch it of course." In that same entry she says simply, "I set our wedding day for April 20th."

January 31, Monday, "Lots of engrossing, so I went up and got crackers, cheese, apples and canned chicken for lunch and took to the office as we didn't have time to go home."

One of the ongoing political discussions had to do with the location of the territorial capitol. From the beginning of the territory in 1863-64 the capitol had been established at Prescott but not without contention from Tucson. In 1867 it was moved to Tucson and then back to Prescott in 1877. In 1889 the capitol was moved a final time to Phoenix.

Angie's diary entry February 9: "Big supper given tonight to the members in favor of Prescott retaining the capitol. George went but came home early, 5 minutes of 11, greatly to my surprise."

Some of the shenanigans that were going on are reflected in entries such as this one on February 10, "House met in morning and adjourned at 1 until 2:20; met and adjourned till 6. Met again at 6 and they `put up a job' to move the Capitol. George Steadman and Wallenberg and the outside members friendly to Prescott, who were in the minority, bolted so there would not be a quorum. The Sergeant at Arms and his assistant caught Harry Woods of Cochise but he broke away from them and jumped out of the window and ran. Fickas, another friend of Yavapai, succeeded in adjourning the Council. George came home at 8:30." [2]

The achievements of the 11th Territorial Legislature were highlighted by the creation of the three new counties: Cochise, Gila and Graham. There was much contention from other towns and objection to the name of Cochise "due to the depredation and murderous attacks of that bloodthirsty savage." Angie prepared those bills with their many amendments and changes. Also there was the incorporation of three towns, Phoenix, Prescott and Tombstone. The Prescott newspaper, always fascinated by the attractive Angie, reported, "Miss Angie Mitchell, with her acceded ability in penmanship, accomplished the very wonderful task of enrolling the Tombstone incorporation act in a little over 18 hours."

During this legislative session the House of Representatives passed a bill on February 16 to move the capitol back to Tucson. After Angie engrossed it, she records on March 19th, "Council finally killed removal of the Capitol on the 12th. At midnight on the 12th the Legislature adjourned."

By the middle of March, with the April 20th wedding date approaching, she had to catch her rest in short snatches between long hours enrolling bills. Her wedding dress, apparently mail ordered, arrived March 15th, "in good condition despite the storms." There had been much snow and winter weather. She wrote, "Between times I've sewed on my wedding clothes."

On Wednesday April 20, 1881 Angeline B. Mitchell was married to the Honorable George E. Brown at the Mitchell home in Prescott. The officiating pastor was Rev. Mr. Hunt of the Congregational church, identified by the *Prescott Weekly Miner* as a "preacher whom they had enjoyed hearing." Their wedding night was spent near the Agua Fria ranch at the home of a neighbor. However, they were discovered and the paper reported, "The happy pair were serenaded by the citizens, all the instruments were of the same kind, tin drums."

For all practical purposes Angie's diary ends with her wedding. The Brown/Mitchell collection at the Sharlot Hall Museum contains numerous scraps of paper on which she has written notes, such as this impersonal line, "Apr. 20, '81, Geo B. and Angie M. married." The archive also contains numerous lists of dated events in Prescott and Yavapai County along with notes about individuals and lists of personal possessions and the artifacts she collected.

The *Daily Arizona Democrat* wrote, "So our friend Brown has become a bridegroom, a much more reputable position than as a Republican member of the Legislature."

The Republican leaning *Weekly Miner* was more generous in an article on April 22. "Mr. Brown was a member of our last Legislature, where he distinguished himself by his honest and upright course on all matters of public interest. He was above petty legislation, and marked out a true, upright and proper course, which he pursued through the session...." The paper was equally generous regarding Angie. "The newly elect Mrs. Brown has been, since her advent into Arizona seven years ago, a teacher of music and schools; has held positions as clerk in the legislatures of the Territory, and in none of her duties has she been remiss or derelict, but always did her work up *brown*. May their ship ever run smooth, never founder or sink, but keep above the silvery surf, and may the Brown family and name... continue to increase and flourish until finally the White House at Washington will be occupied by President Brown, is our wish, and should that person be a son of George and Angie, so much the better."

In 1904 George was appointed to the Maricopa Indian Reservation as an agricultural specialist and superintendent of irrigation. Angie's mother, now a widow, went to live with them and in the summer of 1906 died at the age of 82. Two years later, in March

1908, George contracted spinal meningitis and died. He was 62 years old. The following year Angie died, January 23, 1909. She was 54 years old. Both George and Angie are buried in Phoenix. [3]

NOTES:

[1] 1932 history of the Golden Rule Chapter #1, Eastern Star, an unpublished manuscript, vertical file "Masons", Sharlot Hall Museum archives.
[2] To "put up a job" was slang for arranging a scheme or plot. The Council was the upper chamber of the Legislature ie: the Senate.
[3] Burial places for George and Angie have escaped this historian's searches. There is a George E. Brown buried in the Rosedale Cemetery in Phoenix, part of the Pioneer Military Park. However, public records list his date of death as Nov. 21, 1904, not at all correct for "our" George Brown.

THE END

Photographic Credits

Front Cover: (Angeline Mitchell) Courtesy of Sharlot Hall Museum
Sketch from Angeline Mitchell's Diary: Courtesy of Sharlot Hall Museum
Spring Wagon: *Farm Implement News*, January 1889
Camp Reno: Courtesy of Stan Brown
David & Josephie Harer with David Jr.: Courtesy of Stan Brown
Mile Marker 13: Courtesy of Sandy Carson
Mazatzal City Site: Courtesy of Stan Brown
Doll Baby Ranch Site: Courtesy of Stan Brown
Tonto Creek: Courtesy of Stan Brown
Pole House: Public domain
Headstones: Courtesy of Sandy Carson
Camp Reno 2013: Courtesy of Sandy Carson
Reno Springs: Courtesy of Sandy Carson
Ft. McDowell 2013: Courtesy of Sandy Carson
Adna Chaffee — Public domain
Tonto Creek in Flood: Courtesy of NGCHS, Inc.
Apaches — Stan Brown Collection
Tonto Cliff Dwellings: Courtesy of NGCHS, Inc. (Anna Mae Deming Collection)

Map: Created by Sandy Whalen
Back Cover: Sketch courtesy of Donn Morris

INDEX

76 Ranch, 34
A-Cross Ranch, 40
Adams Ranch, 34
Adams, Texas, 34
Adams, Cordelia, 34
Adams, Emma, 34
Adams, James Monroe
 "Jack" "Cap", 34 *f*, 48
Adams, Jeff, 34
Adams, John A., 34
Adams, John Quincy, 34
Agua Fria River, 132, 141
Allison, "Big Windy", 38
Antelope Mountain, 135
Apache County, 12, 35
Apache Indians, 9, 13, 18, 26, 29, 43, 49*ff*, 67, 69*ff*, 80, 86, 122
Arizona As It Is; The Coming Country, 2
Arizona Mining Association, 7
Armer, Bud, 110*f*
Armer, Frank, 39*f*, 41, 110
Armer, Henry & Lucinda, 39, 108, 114
Armer, James
 see Bud Armer
Armer, Melinda, 39*f*, 115
Armer, Sarah, 39, 103, 108, 115
Armer, Tom, 39*f*, 41, 110
Armer Gulch, 39
Armer Ranch 114
"Arnica Montana", 75
Battle of Big Dry Wash, 49, 122, 127

Blake, Andrew, 24*f*, 86*f*
Blake, Janie, 24, 27, 33, 37, 43*f* 48, 50*ff*, 58*f*, 72, 78, 86*f*
Blake, John, 24
Blake, Narsisses Jane Harer, 24*ff*, 29, 33, 36*f*, 43*ff* 48, 50, 80, 86, 87
Blake, William Garfield, 45
Blake Ranch, 24*f*, 31
Bradshaw Mountains, 6
Brattleboro Vermont Academy, 7
Brown Ranch, 25
Brown, George E., 12, 15*ff*, 22*ff*, 26*f*, 68, 135, 138, 140*ff*
Bullion Tax, 142
Cactus Mountain, 106
Calderwood, Captain M. N., 144
Calderwood's Station, 132
California Volunteers, 132
Callen, Anson W., 7
Camp Bowie, 42
Camp (Fort) McDowell, 66, 73, 120*ff*
Camp Reno, 13, 29, 62, 65, 80, 119
Campbell & Mee's Hall, 4
Campbell, Melton, 26
Chaffee, Adna R., 66, 122*ff*
Chaffee, Annie, 122*ff*
Chilson, Mary Margaret, 111
Chino Valley, 8
Cholla Cactus, 112*f*
Christmas, 117*f*, 124, 129*ff*
Cliff Dwellings, 9, 108*ff*, 146
Cline, Christian, 35, 49

INDEX

Cline, John, 100
Cline, Margaret, 35
Cline, Thomas Jefferson, 34f, 40, 47, 80
Cochise County, 142
Congregational Church, 143
Cook, James, 42
Cottonwood Camp, 6
Crabtree Margaret Alice (Mattie), 34, 36, 38, 80f
Crabtrees', 34, 80, 89, 102
Cordin, Louis, 33
Crawford, Bush, 34
Crook Military Road, 15
Daily Arizona Democrat, 144
Danforths, 47, 49, 110, 116
Doll Baby Ranch, 63
East Clear Creek, 49
East Verde River, 18f, 20, 23
Engrossing, 140, 142
Enrolling, 140, 143f
Fleury, Judge, 3
Fort McDowell
  see Camp McDowell
Fowler, John, 101
Fowler, Tom, 101
Fuller, Elijah Knapp, 18f, 63
Fuller, Mrs., 21f, 63
Garfield, James A., President, 82
Garner, Annie Leah, 35
Genung's, 137
Gila County, 40, 87, 111, 115
Gila Monster, 9, 97ff
Globe, 49, 87, 116
Globe Cemetery, 48
Globe District, 44

Goodwin, Governor, 3
Government Hill, 16
Government Wells, 17
Graham County, 142
Granite Creek, 3, 5, 138
Granite Creek (street), 140
Grapevine Springs, 39
Green Valley, 18f, 22f, 27
Greenback Creek, 34, 37
Greenback Valley, 13f, 34, 37, 43f, 85, 87
Groves, Rev., 5
Hance, George & Parthena, 15f
Hancock, W.A. (William Augustus), 13f, 43, 47, 85, 101, 130, 133
Hardt, Henrich Frederic Christian, 86
Harer, Alice Lucinda, 44f, 47, 50f, 59, 69f, 72ff, 80, 83, 87f, 93, 95, 100, 102, 108, 113
Harer, Clara Belle, 42, 46ff, 69f, 73, 78, 80, 83, 87ff, 95, 99, 102, 108, 112ff
Harer Family, 14, 37, 40, 43ff, 82, 85ff, 117, 124, 131
Harer Ranch, 34
Harer, David, 14, 24, 33, 37f, 42, 44, 80, 82, 100, 118, 120ff, 130
Harer, David Corwin Asbury Gleason "Abbie," 12, 45, 65, 85, 87, 88
Harer, Annie Eliza, 86
Harer, Evan, 85

INDEX

Harer, James, 80*ff*, 100
Harer, Josephine, 33, 37, 42, 46*ff*, 50*f*, 57*f*, 72, 74*ff*, 81, 88*ff*, 93, 95, 106, 117, 125*f*
Harer, Mary Elizabeth
　see Vineyard
Harer, Nathaniel Green, 37, 82, 85, 90
Harer, Newton Green, 86
Harer, Obedience McClendon, 85
Harer, Redman, 85, 100*f*
Harer, Sarah Frances Lincoln, 87
Hazelton, Carter, 90, 100*f*
Hazelton, Charles, 90
Hazelton, George, 88
Hazelton, Laura, 88, 90
Hazleton, Ida, 88, 90
Hazelton, Obedience, 85*f*, 90, 101, 108, 117*f*, 120, 125
Hedgpeth, Rev., 5
Hieroglyphic, 111
Hodge, Hiram C., 2
Hook, Belle, 34*f*, 38, 78, 83, 88*f*, 101
Hook, James & Rebecca, 35, 38, 44, 69*f*, 77*f*, 80, 101, 107*f*, 117*ff*
Hook, Leah, 35, 40
Hook Ranch, 119
Howard, Mary, 48
Hunt, Rev., 143
"Hydrophobia cat," 83
Kansas State Agricultural College, 7

Lindsay, Pascal Augustua, 87
Lost Dutchman Mining Association, 133
Lower Tonto, 31, 34, 36, 39, 73
Lower Tonto School, 31
Mazatzal City, 63
Mazatzal Mountains, 85
McClendon, Obedience
　see Harer
Merrill, Rev. J.A., 6
Methodist Episcopal Church, 5
Methodist Mountain, 40, 87
Miles, Andy, 15
Miller Valley, 8
Mitchell County, Kansas, 8
Mitchell, Daniel Francis, 8*f*
Mitchell, William D., 7*f*
Mogollon Rim, 12, 16, 20, 49, 122
Moore, George, 117, 121
Mormon Dam, 121
Mormon Flat, 121
Mormons, 17, 121
Mt. Ord, 29
Mud Tanks, 16, 20
Narrows, The, 25*f*
Nash Point, 17
Nellie Boyd Troupe, 133
North Fork, 26
O'Leary, Dan, 12
Old Camp Reno
　see Camp Reno
Onyx (dog), 118*f*, 131, 133, 135, 138, 142

INDEX

Ox Bow Hill, 23
Packard, Florence, 37, 87
Papago Indians, 51, 54
Payson, 19, 40, 67, 111
Pemberton's, 45
Persons, William, 39, 44*ff*
Phoenix, 8, 12*f*, 43, 66, 68, 70, 77, 85, 101*f*, 117*f*, 24, 129*ff*, 138, 142*f*, 146
Pine, AZ, *18f*, 23, 28
Pleasant Valley, 40
Pole House, 9, 36, 59, 64, 82, 91*ff*
Prather Brothers, 29, 119
Prather, Isaac R., 119
Prather, William, 29
Prescott, 1*ff*, 12*f*, 26, 29, 42, 45, 87, 89, 100*ff*, 108, 115, 117, 122, 129*ff*, 135, 138, 140*ff*
Prescott Free Academy, 15
Prescott Weekly Miner, 1, 4, 6, 14, 133, 144*f*
Punkin Center, 29
Raible, Mrs., 4
Reeder, Rev. G.A., 88
Reno Hill, 119
Reno Mountain, 87
Richmond Basin, 49, 116
Roosevelt Dam, 34
Roosevelt Lake, 34, 40, 111, 115
Rothrock, George H., 130
Rupert, Mrs. E. M., 131*ff*
Rye Creek, 16, 22*ff*, 26, 31, 36
Rye, AZ, 23
Salt River, 39, 108, 121

Salt River Valley, 13
San Carlos Agency, 71
San Carlos Reservation, 26, 49*ff*, 67, 122
Saratoga (trunk), 131
Sharlot Hall Museum, 1, 9*f*, 25, 29, 87, 144, 146*f*
Sharp, Captain, 130
Sherman, Professor Moses H., 3, 13, 15
Sierra Ancha, 13, 85, 103
Skunk, Mr., 82
St. Johns, Apache County, 12
Stanton, Charles B., 133
Stanton Station, 133, 135
Stations, 38
Steadman, George, 143
Stephens, Josie, 10
Strawberry, AZ, 17, 28
Sunflower Mountain, 119
Sunflower Valley, 119
Surprise, AZ, 132
Tatman, John, 1
Tempe, 125, 129
Tempe News, 25, 87
Territorial Board of Examiners for Teachers, 8
Territorial Capital, 8, 16, 100
Territorial Certificate, 13, 15
Territorial Legislature, 2, 1 108, 117, 133, 140, 143
Territorial Prison, 40, 111
Territorial School Superintendent, 15
The History of Tonto, 37, 82
The Miner, 5, 10

151

INDEX

Tiger Mine, 8
Tombstone, 143
Tonto Academy, 46
Tonto Apache Indians, 26, 49, 122
Tonto Creek, 14, 22, 24*ff*, 31, 34, 36, 39, 61, 64, 67, 70, 77, 103, 140
Tonto National Monument, 68, 115
Tonto Road, 12
Tonto School, 13, 31, 43, 50, 85, 85, 97, 115
Tucson, 142, 145
United States Land Office, 7
Ute Mountain, 109, 115
Verde River, 3, 18, 120*ff*
Verde Valley, 16
Vineyard, Agnes, 33, 36
Vineyard, Ezra, 33, 36
Vineyard, Green, 33, 36, 47
Vineyard, John, 33*f*, 36, 51, 69*f*, 86, 107, 118, 121*f*
Vineyard, Johnny, 33, 36, 46*f*, 69
Vineyard, Mary Elizabeth, 33, 43, 45*f*, 59, 69, 86
Vineyard, Willie, 33, 39, 44, 46, 69, 73, 98*f*
Wallenberg, 143
Walnut Grove, 6, 8
Walnut Grove School, 6
Weekly Miner
  see *Prescott Weekly Miner*
West Side Church, 141
Whipple Barracks, 101

Whiskey Row, 141
White Mountain Apaches, 71
White Mountain Reservation, 49*f*, 122
Wickenburg, 132*f*, 135
Wickiup, 13
Wild Rye Creek
  see Rye Creek
Woods, Harry, 143
Yavapai County, 2*f*, 5*f*, 8*f*, 15, 95, 140, 144
Yavapai Indians, 29, 143
Yuma, 40, 111
Zuni Indians, 109